T5-DHJ-594

The Supernatural Power of Jesus

The Supernatural Power of Jesus

by
John MacArthur, Jr.

MOODY PRESS
CHICAGO

© 1984, 1985 by
JOHN MACARTHUR, JR.

All rights reserved. No part of this book may be reproduced in any form
without permission in writing from the publisher, except in the case of brief
quotations embodied in critical articles or reviews.

All Scripture quotations, unless otherwise noted, are from the *New Scofield
Reference Bible*, King James Version, © 1967 by Oxford University Press, Inc.
Reprinted by permission.

Moody Press, a ministry of the Moody Bible Institute, is designed for
education, evangelization, and edification. If we may assist you in knowing more about Christ and the Christian life, please write us without
obligation: Moody Press, c/o MLM, Chicago, Illinois 60610.

ISBN: 0-8024-5113-6
1 2 3 4 5 6 7 Printing/GB/Year 90 89 88 87 86 85

Printed in the United States of America

Contents

1

Jesus' Power over Disease— Part 1

Outline

Introduction
A. The Setting of Christ's Miracles in Matthew
  1. An affirmation of Christ's deity
  2. An answer to the debate
B. The Significance of Christ's First Miracles in Matthew
  1. He begins at the lowest level of human need
  2. He compassionately responds to appeals
  3. He acts on His own will
  4. He graciously approaches the lowly in society

Lesson
I. The Wretched Man
  A. The Attraction to the Lord
  B. The Analysis of the Leprosy
    1. The nature of leprosy
    2. The instructions about leprosy
      a) The process of identifying leprosy
        (1) The scripture about the disease
        (2) The seriousness of the disease
        (3) The symptoms of the disease
      b) The purposes for isolating leprosy
  C. The Approach of the Leper
    1. His confidence
    2. His reverence
    3. His humility
    4. His faith
  D. The Acting of the Lord
    1. The hand of healing
      a) Its simplicity
      b) Its suddenness
    2. The command for cleansing
      a) Its procedure
      b) Its purpose

Conclusion
A. The Characteristics of Conversion
B. The Consequence of Conversion

Introduction

A. The Setting of Christ's Miracles in Matthew

1. An affirmation of Christ's deity

Chapters eight through twelve of Matthew are critical to the understanding of the life of Christ and the message of Matthew. In that section, Matthew records nine of the countless miracles performed by Jesus Christ as examples of His power. Those miracles are His credentials as the Messiah—signs that point convincingly to His deity, for only God can do the things that He did. The sad part is that after the miracles in chapters 8 and 9 and the preaching that follows them, the Jewish leaders conclude that Jesus is of the devil in chapter 12. Matthew shows that Christ had done everything possible to manifest His deity, but the leaders conclude exactly the opposite. As a result, He turns from the Jewish religious structure toward the establishment of a Gentile church in chapter 13.

Notice that chapter 8 begins with three miracles of healing that involve a leper in verses 2-4, a man with paralysis in verses 5-13, and a woman with a fever in verses 14-15. Those form the opening triad of miracles among the nine miracles in chapters 8 and 9. There are three sections of miracles, each section containing three miracles followed by a response. Those miracles manifest the deity of Jesus Christ by demonstrating creative power that can only be attributed to God. They are the credentials of the King—proof that He is divine.

2. An answer to the debate

The first section of miracles comes at a very strategic point in the gospel of Matthew, because Jesus has just delivered a blistering sermon in chapters 5 through 7. He had turned the Jewish religious world topsy-turvy by saying that its teachings, attitudes, and actions were wrong. Much of what the Jewish people believed in and hoped for was wrong. Unlike other teachers, Jesus never bothered to quote any rabbis or any of their well-known sources of authority. He affirmed the truth by repeatedly saying, "Ye have heard that it was said . . . but I say . . ." (Matt. 5:21-22; cf. vv. 27-28, 33-34, 38-39, 43-44). Matthew records the people's reaction to Jesus' sermon in 7:28-29: "And it came to pass, when Jesus had ended these sayings, the people were astonished at his doctrine; for he taught them as one having authority, and not as the scribes." The rabbis quoted other fallible rabbis to support their material, but Jesus merely spoke without quoting any source. In so doing, He unmasked them as spiritual phonies.

This brings up some very pointed questions. A Jewish person in the first century probably would have wondered, *Who is saying these things? By what authority does He speak? Why should we believe what He's saying?* Chapters 8 and 9 provide the answers to those questions. The fact that Christ is God and can perform miracles is proof that He had the right to speak as He did. In the person of Jesus we see God at work.

B. The Significance of Christ's First Miracles in Matthew

Matthew records four key things about the first three miracles that Jesus performed.

1. He begins at the lowest level of human need

Jesus treated the physical problems of people. Although life consists of more than just the physical, Jesus *is* sympathetic about that realm. It's wonderful that the miracles of Jesus not only dealt with spiritual things, but with physical things as well, as they touch man at his most immediate level of recognized need. In the first set of miracles, Jesus confronted human disease, whereas in the second set, He dealt more with spiritual problems. By showing that Christ met the lowest level of human needs, Matthew shows the sympathy of Christ in addition to His power.

2. He compassionately responds to appeals

In the first miracle of healing, the leper says, "Lord, if thou wilt, thou canst make me clean" (Matt. 8:2*b*). In the second miracle, Jesus agrees to heal the centurion's servant, saying, "I will come and heal him" (8:7). In the third miracle, according to what Luke adds in the parallel passage, friends of Peter's family request Jesus to come and heal Peter's mother-in-law, and He does. In all three cases He responds to the appeals from the hearts of people.

3. He acts on His own will

Although Jesus is sympathetic and deeply compassionate, He is also sovereign. In each case, He acted on His own volition, saying, "I will, be thou clean" (v. 3); "I will come and heal him" (v. 7); "And he touched her hand, and the fever left her" (v. 15).

4. He graciously approaches the lowly in society

In each of these miracles, Jesus touches someone who was considered to be at the lowest level of human existence. First, a leper; second, a Gentile; and third, a woman. The subtlety of His interaction with such individuals devastated the pride of the Pharisees. Jesus put His emphasis on the humble and the outcast. In fact, the first person He ever revealed His messiahship to was a harlot in Samaria who wasn't even Jewish! That was a shock to the Jewish society of His day.

From the very start, Jesus made clear that He was going to establish His authority by miraculous power. Yet, with all His willingness to compassionately heal the helpless of society, the Jewish leaders turned their backs on Him. In chapter 12 we find them concluding that the miracles He accomplishes are done by the power of Beelzebub, the prince of demons. In fact, they hated Him so much, they sought to kill Him because He upset their religious security.

They refused to accept the abundant evidence of His divine power. He cleansed a leper, healed a servant, raised up a woman, controlled the sea, cast out demons, made the blind see, the crippled walk, the dumb speak, and healed every sickness that was brought to Him.

In the flow of Matthew's narrative, chapter 8 begins where chapter 4 left off: "And Jesus went about all Galilee, teaching in their synagogues, and preaching the gospel of the kingdom, and healing all manner of sickness and all manner of disease among the people. And his fame went throughout all Syria; and they brought unto him all sick people that were taken with diverse diseases and torments, and those who were possessed with demons, and those who were epileptics, and those who had the palsy [paralysis]; and he healed them. And there followed him great multitudes of people from Galilee, and from Decapolis, and from Jerusalem, and from Judea, and from beyond the Jordan" (4:23-25). Then, in the midst of His healing ministry, Jesus preached the Sermon on the Mount, came down and again started healing uncounted numbers of people who came to Him.

Lesson

I. THE WRETCHED MAN (vv. 1-4)

"When he was come down from the mountain, great multitudes followed him. And, behold, there came a leper and worshiped him, saying, Lord, if thou wilt, thou canst make me clean. And Jesus put forth his hand, and touched him, saying, I will; be thou clean. And immediately his leprosy was cleansed. And Jesus saith unto him, See thou tell no man, but go thy way, show thyself to the priest, and offer the gift that Moses commanded, for a testimony unto them."

A. The Attraction to the Lord (v. 1)

"When he was come down from the mountain, great multitudes followed him."

Jesus came down from a mountain near the village of Capernaum after He had finished preaching His sermon. Many people continued to follow Him, but not because they loved Him or believed in Him; they were curious about His unique authority. They had never heard anybody speak in such a manner or heal people so miraculously. As a result, a huge crowd was attracted to Jesus and followed Him to see what other things He would do.

B. The Analysis of the Leprosy (v. 2a)

"And, behold, there came [lit., "approached"] a leper."

What is unusual about this scene is that a leper wouldn't normally dare to approach someone, but this one did. To better understand why, let us examine

1. The nature of leprosy

The word "leper" is from the Greek word *lepros,* which comes from the root word *lepis,* which means "scale." In the Old Testa-

10

ment, there is a Hebrew word that is translated leprosy that also means "scale." In both cases, leprosy referred to the scaly skin that was one symptom of the disease, though it could go much deeper than that. There is a lot of debate about whether the leprosy of the Bible was the same as what we know today as Hansen's Disease. We can't be sure because diseases can take on new forms over the centuries as people build up immunities for them. It seems best to assume from the description of Leviticus 13 that it was very similar. The only real comparison we can draw to the biblical disease will come from our understanding of modern leprosy.

Leprosy found its way into the lives of the children of Israel. That horrible disease was evidently picked up in Egypt. Some classical sources mention that leprosy originated in Egypt, and the disease has been found in at least one mummified body that was discovered there. Leprosy might have been transmitted to the children of Israel when they were in the land of Egypt and carried with them into the Promised Land. God designed many laws for Israel to protect them from contracting and speading such diseases as leprosy. Modern-day leprosy, now known to be caused by bacteria called *mycobaterium leprae,* is communicable to less than 10 percent of the world's population. In other words, at least 90 percent of people in our day cannot contract leprosy. However, it appears that in ancient times the disease was more communicable. For example, Jesus says in Luke 4:27 that "many lepers were in Israel in the time of Elisha, the prophet; and none of them was cleansed, but only Naaman, the Syrian." But today, even though leprosy is on the rise in the United States and apparently can't be eliminated, it can be controlled by a drug called *Dapsone.*

2. The instructions about leprosy

In Leviticus 13, God gave Israel very clear directions regarding

   a) The process of identifying leprosy

      (1) The scripture about the disease

         "Then the Lord spoke to Moses and to Aaron, saying, When a man has on the skin of his body a swelling or a scab [rash] or a bright spot, and it becomes an infection of leprosy on the skin of his body, then he shall be brought to Aaron the priest, or to one of his sons the priests. And the priest shall look at the mark on the skin of the body, and if the hair in the infection has turned white and the infection appears to be deeper than the skin of his body, it is an infection of leprosy; when the priest has looked at him, he shall pronounce him unclean. But if the bright spot is white on the skin of his body, and it does not appear to be deeper than the skin, and the hair on it has not turned white, then the priest shall isolate him who has the infection for seven days. And the priest shall look at him on the seventh day, and if in his eyes the infection has not changed, the infection has not spread on the skin, then the priest shall isolate him for seven more days. And the priest shall look at him again on the seventh day; and if the infection has faded, and the mark has not spread on the skin, then the priest shall pronounce him clean; it is only a [rash (possibly psoriasis or eczema)]. And he shall wash his clothes and be clean. But if the [rash] spreads farther on the skin, after he has shown himself to the priest for his cleansing, he shall appear again to the priest. And the priest shall look, and if the [rash] has spread on the skin, then the priest shall pronounce him unclean; it is leprosy. When the infection of leprosy is on a man, then he shall be brought to the priest. The priest shall then look, and if there is a white swelling in the skin, and it has turned the hair white, and there is quick raw flesh in the swelling, it is a chronic leprosy on the skin of his body, and the priest shall pronounce him unclean; he shall not isolate him, for he is unclean. And if the leprosy breaks out farther on the skin, and the leprosy covers all the skin of him who has the infection from his head even to his feet, as far as the priest can see, then the priest shall look, and behold, if the leprosy has covered all his body, he shall pronounce clean him who has the infection; it has all turned white and he is clean" (vv. 1-13; NASB*).

In other words, if the skin just turns white, but doesn't break out in open, raw sores, then it isn't a serious form of leprosy. Herodotus and Hippocrates in their ancient writings wrote about a disease known as *leukodermia,* which was an infection that attacked the pigmentation of the skin and turned it a patchy white color. Such symptoms could have been evidence of eczema, psoriasis, or any relatively harmless skin disorder, including the mild form of leprosy known as "tuberculoid," which may last for one to three years.

(2) The seriousness of the disease

A person who had the severe kind of leprosy, which we identify as *lepromatous,* had to follow the instructions at the end of Leviticus 13: "As for the leper who has the infection, his clothes shall be torn, and the hair of his head shall be uncovered, and he shall cover his mustache and cry, 'Unclean! Unclean!' " (v. 45; NASB).

A *Los Angeles Times* article on the medical analysis of Hansen's disease stated that leprosy can be passed on to others when it is inhaled through the air. That is a good reason for a leper to cover his mouth. People have also

New American Standard Bible.

contracted leprosy when they have both touched the same object. For example, there are cases where people who have been tattooed with the same needle become infected with the same kind of leprosy. That is why Leviticus 13 instructed a person who had the severe kind of leprosy to do away with his garments. As long as he had that infection, he had to cover his face and make an announcement of his presence so that no one would get near him. In fact, the Talmud forbade a Jew from getting any closer than six feet to a leper, and if there was a wind blowing, one hundred and fifty feet was the limit. Of the sixty-one defilements in Judaism, the most serious was contacting a dead body and next to that was being infected with leprosy. Consequently, people didn't go near lepers, let alone touch them. In a very important article on the Old Testament word for leprosy, R. K. Harrison points out that all of the symptoms of Leviticus 13 "could presage clinical leprosy" (Colin Brown, ed. *The New International Dictionary of New Testament Theology, vol. 2* [Grand Rapids: Zondervan, 1967], p. 465). Therefore, the tests of Leviticus were needed to distinguish between different skin infections so that in obvious cases of leprosy, the person could be put out.

(3) The symptoms of the disease

Serious leprosy is a terrible disease as indicated:

The disease which we today call leprosy generally begins with pain in certain areas of the body. Numbness follows. Soon the skin in such spots loses its original color. It gets to be thick, glossy, and scaly. . . . As the sickness progresses, the thickened spots become dirty sores and ulcers due to poor blood supply. The skin, especially around the eyes and ears, begins to bunch, with deep furrows between the swellings, so that the face of the afflicted individual begins to resemble that of a lion. Fingers drop off or are absorbed; toes are affected similarly. Eyebrows and eyelashes drop out. By this time one can see the person in this pitiable condition is a leper. By a touch of the finger one can also feel it. One can even smell it, for the leper emits a very unpleasant odor. Moreover, in view of the fact that the disease-producing agent frequently also attacks the larynx, the leper's voice acquires a grating quality. "His throat becomes hoarse, and you can now not only see, feel, and smell the leper, but you can hear his rasping voice. And if you stay with him for some time, you can even imagine a peculiar taste in your mouth, probably due to the odor" (L. S. Huizenga, *Unclean! Unclean!* [Grand Rapids: 1927], p. 149; as cited by W. Hendriksen in *The Gospel of Matthew* [Grand Rapids: Baker, 1973], p. 388.

13

b) The purposes for isolating leprosy

All the human senses naturally would be repulsed at a person who suffered from this horrifying disease. Whether or not it could attack the total population or only a few people, a leper had to be sent out of the camp to protect the health of others. In 2 Samuel 3:29, David curses the house of Joab that it might never be without a leper. That was evidently one of the worst things that could be said to someone, especially since the disease had no cure.

Because of the physical ugliness of the disease, God had a spiritual purpose in marking out lepers as ceremonially unclean. Leprosy was a most graphic illustration of the sin that defiles the whole body. Sin is ugly, loathsome, incurable, and contaminating; it separates men from God and makes them outcasts. Every leper not only lived with the stigma of his own disease, but also with the stigma of being a walking illustration of sin. In fact, one rabbi in the Talmud said that when he saw lepers, he flung stones at them to keep them away. Another rabbi said that he would not even eat an egg bought in a street where a leper had passed by. In this light, isn't it shocking that Jesus began presenting the credentials of His messiahship by healing a leper and not some sick Pharisee in town?

Let's look at Jesus' first specific healing recorded in Matthew.

C. The Approach of the Leper (v. 2)

1. His confidence (v. 2*a*)

"And, behold, there came [approached] a leper."

After all that we have seen regarding leprosy, it is clear that lepers wouldn't dare approach another person to communicate with him. Such an act was unthinkable, shameful, and contrary to Old Testament law. You will remember that a leper was required to announce his presence by covering his mouth and saying, "Unclean, unclean," so that no one would come near. But the very fact that this leper approached Jesus shows us that he came with confidence. He didn't crawl or sneak around and try to whisper from behind a bush to get Jesus' attention; he came right up to Him. I can imagine that much of that crowd left in a hurry. I see here a man who so desperately sensed his need, he didn't care what others thought. Normally, people in his condition would be so socially devastated that they wouldn't show up in a crowd, but this leper lost all sense of shame and social stigma. That's how deep his need was. Josephus, the ancient historian, tells us that lepers were treated like dead men. But that wasn't going to stop him. He may have been dead in everybody else's eyes, but he still came, because he recognized that his need was beyond his power to remedy, and he wanted help more than he wanted to save his reputation.

2. His reverence (v. 2b)

"And worshiped him, saying, Lord."

We may not be able to say much about his appearance, but we can say a lot about his soul. In stark contrast to the Pharisees—who were arrayed in their fancy garbs and had their beards perfectly trimmed, but were spiritually wretched on the inside (Matt. 23:27-28)—stood the leper. He was wretched and filthy on the outside, yet beautifully reverent on the inside. I believe when he said "Lord," he wasn't using it in the sense of "Sir." Rather, he acknowledged that he was in the presence of God, because he fell prostrate before Jesus to worship Him (Gk., *proskuein*). I don't know where that leper got his information about Christ, but there had been enough healings going on in his area for him to know that Jesus was not just a man. He came and worshiped in a way men come before kings and God. I believe he came because he had a worshiping heart. He was in the presence of God, and he knew it. It is wonderful to see that his soul was turned toward God in worship because he understood that the soul was more important than the body. Before he sought anything for himself, he exalted God.

3. His humility (v. 2c)

"If thou wilt."

The leper didn't demand anything—he didn't speak his will as if Christ had to comply, listing the reasons he had to be healed. He didn't try to affirm his own worthiness or bellyache because he had a disease that other folks didn't. He didn't talk about his rights or even about his desires, saying, "I'd like to be healed." He only said, "If You wanted to heal me, You could. I'm not saying what You ought to do, because You're the Lord." That's a far cry from what you hear today when people are told to demand healing from God by "claiming" it. This man, however, made no such claim— he worshiped first, never asking for anything. I agree with the commentator Lenski, that the leper was willing to accept Jesus' choice for him to remain in his "living death" if He had so willed (*The Interpretation of St. Matthew's Gospel* [Minneapolis: Augsburg, 1964], p. 319). In that event, I believe that he would have gone away still believing in Jesus, or he wouldn't have worshiped first and left out any request on his own behalf. That man manifested a pure heart.

4. His faith (v. 2d)

"Thou canst make me clean."

The word for "canst" in the Greek is *dunasai*. It is the term that the word *dynamite* is derived from. Appropriately, it means "to have power." The leper, who was "full of leprosy" (according to Luke, the doctor [5:12]), was convinced that Jesus had the power to heal him. Maybe he knew that because he had been around when Jesus was healing in Matthew 4. When a man says, "If You

15

will, You can do it," he illustrates faith at its highest point, because he knows that God is able, and submits to His sovereignty. There are lots of people who *say* they believe He is able, but they want to corner Him to accomplish their desires. There are other people who question whether He can. But a true man of faith says, "I know You can; I just don't know if You will." That's the highest level of faith.

So the leper came with confidence because he had a deep need; he came with reverence because he saw God; he came with humility because he realized that God was sovereign; and he came with faith, because he knew that Jesus could heal him.

D. The Acting of the Lord (vv. 3-4)

1. The hand of healing (v. 3)

   a) Its simplicity (v. 3*a*)

   "And Jesus put forth his hand, and touched him."

   That is about all it says in the text, but it could be added that the whole crowd gasped—Jesus had touched a leper! That was seemingly contrary to Leviticus 5:3, which prohibited anyone from touching "the uncleanness of man." But a touch from someone clean was probably what that leper needed more than anything else. Jesus touched him, though He didn't have to. He could have stood on a roof and said, "Be clean!" as angels sang, the earth shook, and thunder sounded. However, there were no spectacular dramatics.

   b) Its suddenness (v. 3*b*)

   "[Jesus said] I will; be thou clean. And immediately the leprosy was cleansed."

   Essentially all of Jesus' miracles were immediate. It bothers me when people say, "I went to the healer and was healed and have been getting better ever since." That's not healing. Jesus put forth His hand and touched him, and true healing occurred. When we touch a disease, we get contaminated; when He touched a disease, it was cleansed with His power. I can imagine those shriveled-up claws instantly becoming beautiful hands along with the restoration of his face and the rest of his body. Even though leprosy had eaten away the leper's eyebrows and eyelashes, left his skin scaly and bloody, destroyed his nose and throat, and caused his fingers and toes to be worn off, Jesus was able to restore him instantly to his former health. In comparison to that omnipotent display, all the modern "healing" fades into absolute nothingness. You can line up all the so-called healers in the world, and they can pick out any leper they want, but none of them will be able to do what Jesus did. Let those healers be silent, for their claims are folly in comparison to the power of Christ, who alone is able to recreate parts of the body that have been destroyed.

2. The command for cleansing (v. 4)

"And Jesus saith unto him, See thou tell no man, but go thy way, show thyself to the priest, and offer the gift that Moses commanded, for a testimony unto them."

a) Its procedure

What is the first evidence that Christ has entered your life? Obedience. That is why He says, "Now that you've been healed, do what Moses commanded in the law of God." In the unlikely event that a leper was healed, Leviticus 14 gave instructions about the ceremony for his cleansing at the Temple. First of all, he had to take two birds and kill one of them over running water. The other was dipped in the blood of the first bird along with cedar wood, a scarlet cord, and hyssop (a plant) and then allowed to fly away. That pictured resurrection. Then the former leper washed himself and his clothes, shaved, and waited seven days to be re-examined. Afterwards, he shaved his hair, head, and eyebrows, and sacrificed two male lambs without blemish, one ewe lamb, three tenths of a measure of fine flour mingled with oil, and about a pint of oil. Then the leper was touched on the tip of his right ear, thumb, and big toe with blood and oil. Upon final examination, if the cure was real, the man was given a certificate stating that he had been cleansed.

b) Its purpose

You say, "I can understand that Jesus wanted the leper to obey, because He didn't come to destroy the law but to fulfill it. But why did He instruct him not to tell anybody else?" Some people believe that Jesus didn't want to stir up a crowd that only followed Him because He was a miracle worker. That is very possible, because large crowds made it difficult for Him to function. Others say Jesus said that because He didn't want the people to see Him as someone who could throw off the yoke of Rome as a political leader. You may remember in John 6:15 that the people try to do that very thing. And still others say that Jesus didn't want to seek any exaltation during the time of His humiliation.

There may be truth in all of those suggestions, but let me give you what I think is the best reason. If you read the rest of the verse, you find that he was instructed to appear before the priests "for a testimony unto them." If the leper had gone down to the Temple to participate in the cleansing and eight-day examination required in the Mosaic law, the priests would have had to conclude that he was cleansed. Then, when they discovered that Jesus of Nazareth was responsible for the leper's healing, they would be trapped in their own conclusions. Their own examination would confirm the power of Christ. But that all hinged on the leper's hurrying to Jerusalem without spreading the news, or word would get around that Jesus healed him, and the priests wouldn't be interested in examining him. Unfortunately, the man didn't follow Jesus' instruction, as Mark 1:45 tells us. He became so excited that he failed to obey.

Conclusion

A. The Characteristics of Conversion

Jesus said, "Which is more difficult, to heal disease or forgive sin?" (Mark 2:9). Do you know why He said that? In doing those kinds of miracles, He was not only revealing His power over disease, but also using them as illustrations of His power over sin. I think our text is analogous to a conversion. Leprosy, a ceremonially unclean illness, is a demonstration of sin. Like leprosy, sin is pervasive, ugly, loathsome, communicable, incurable, and makes you an outcast. In spite of that, however, the leper came with confidence, because he was desperate over his leprosy. That's the first step of conversion. People don't get saved unless they are desperate over the loathsomeness of the disease of sin. That element is often missing in the evangelism of our time. The man came, having lost all fear of being ostracized. He was overwhelmed with the loathsomeness of his disease. Coming to Christ is not getting on the bandwagon—it's being wretched and knowing it.

Second, the leper came worshiping. I believe that true conversion occurs when desperate people come worshiping God—not seeking things for themselves, but seeking God's glory. There needs to be a recognition of His majesty, a sense of awe regarding His lordship.

Third, he came humbly. True salvation doesn't take the perspective of doing God a favor. There's no self-will or self-centeredness, no sense of worthiness, and no acknowledgement of rights or claims involved. It's the meek who inherit the kingdom.

Finally, the leper came with faith. He believed that Jesus could heal him. You can't be saved without faith. So, with regard to salvation, you will be touched and cleansed when you come to Christ in faith. And may I add that the disease of sin is infinitely worse than the disease of leprosy.

B. The Consequence of Conversion

Once you're saved, do you know what the Lord asks? "Will you obey the law of God and let people discover for themselves that I have changed your life?" A living testimony can be more effective than a verbal one. It's better for you to say nothing and let the world see that Jesus changed your life than for you to be unable to support what you say with the way you live. Here was a man running around testifying, "Jesus changed my life! Look at me—I used to be a leper, but come and see me now!" Then somebody asks, "Why aren't you showing yourself to the priest?" An answer like, "I'm going to get to that,"

18

could have discredited his testimony. A disobedient life in the midst of a testimony is meaningless; the testimony is rendered invalid. Be obedient, and in the midst of your obedience, God will manifest the transforming power of Christ. Your life speaks louder than words.

Focusing on the Facts

1. Why does Matthew record the miracles of Jesus? What are they credentials of (see p. 8)?

2. Sadly, after Jesus had performed many miracles, what did a number of Jewish leaders conclude in Matthew 12? As a result, what did Jesus do (see p. 8)?

3. What type of miracles are the first three of the nine miracles that are recorded in Matthew 8-9 (see p. 8)?

4. What was unique about Jesus' teaching? What was the reaction of the people to His teaching (Matt. 7:28-29; see p. 8)?

5. What are some significant elements of Christ's healings in Matthew 8 (see p. 9)?

6. After Jesus had preached His Sermon on the Mount, why did many people continue to follow Him (see p. 10)?

7. Where did leprosy apparently originate? When would it have been transmitted to the Israelites (see p. 11)?

8. What is one reason God designed many laws regarding leprosy (see p. 11)?

9. What did a person who had the severe form of leprosy have to do, according to Leviticus 13:45 (see p. 12)?

10. What were considered to be the two most serious defilements in Judaism (see p. 13)?

11. What spiritual purpose did God have in marking out leprosy as ceremonially unclean (see p. 14)?

12 What attitude did the leper manifest in his approach to Jesus (see p. 14)?

13. Why had the leper lost all sense of social stigma (see p. 14)?

14. What did the leper recognize that prompted him to worship Jesus (see pp. 14-15)?

15. How did the leper express his humility (see p. 15)?

16. Even though he was full of leprosy, what was the leper convinced of (see p. 15)?

17. Describe the highest level of faith (see pp. 15-16).

18. How does the healing ministry of Christ differ from the ministries of modern "healers" (see p. 16)?

19. Why did Jesus tell the leper not to tell anyone but the priest of his healing? List a few possible reasons (see p. 17).

20. What is the healing of the leper analogous to? Explain (see p. 18).

21. How can the testimony of a changed life be discredited (see p. 18)?

Pondering the Principles

1. In 1 Corinthians 11:1, Paul says, "Be ye followers of me, even as I also am of Christ," and in Romans 8:29 he says that God desires to conform us us "to the image of his Son." Knowing, then, that we are to become more like Christ within the limitations of our humanity, how can we model ourselves after Him, even though we cannot effect a miraculous cure for someone? Look through the significance of Christ's first miracles in Matthew on pages 0 and 0. List some practical ways you could minister to the physical needs of people in your sphere of influence. Have you compassionately responded to any appeals from those in need? Did you take action independently of others, or did you only respond to the pressure of what others would think if you neglected to help? Though you may not have much interaction with the lowliest in society because of where you work or live, occasionally you do meet those whom others would avoid because of their ethnic background, poverty, or appearance. Keep a lookout with an eye towards ministry for those who may be ignored by society, but are nevertheless loved by God.

2. Does the manner in which the leper worshiped Jesus exemplify your own reverence toward God? Do you approach God in prayer primarily to acknowledge His majesty and seek to know Him more, or is your prayer simply a tool for prying requests out of Him? Read through Daniel's prayer in Daniel 9 for a model of a prayer with the proper perspective.

3. Imagine a life insurance agent who wants to sell you a policy he would never buy himself, or a car salesman who is trying to sell you an American car, but drives a Japanese car. It is hard to have confidence in a person who doesn't believe in what he sells, because his words aren't clearly backed up by his actions. Evaluate your actions—what you say, where you spend your time, and how you do things. Is your testimony enhanced or hindered by any of those things?

2
Jesus' Power over Disease—Part 2

Outline

Introduction
A. Disease in the Time of Christ
  1. Explained
  2. Eliminated
    a) Matthew 12:15
    b) Matthew 14:14
B. Disbelief in the Miracles of Christ

Review
I. The Wretched Man

Lesson
II. The Respected Man
  A. The Place
  B. The Person
    1. A centurion
    2. A Samaritan
  C. The Petition
    1. His respect
    2. His reputation
    3. His reward
    4. His response
      a) Of humility
      b) Of faith
        (1) His knowledge of Jesus' ability
        (2) His knowledge of Jesus' authority
  D. The Praise
    1. Jesus' recognition
    2. Jesus' rebuke
  E. The Prediction
    1. The inclusion of Gentiles in the kingdom
      a) Described
      b) Denied

2. The exclusion of Jews from the kingdom
- *a*) The promise to the Jews
- *b*) The punishment of the Jews
  - (1) The place
  - (2) The pain
    - (*a*) Matthew 13:42
    - (*b*) Matthew 22:13
    - (*c*) Matthew 24:51

F. The Promise

III. The Relative
- A. The Situation
- B. The Sickness
- C. The Service

Introduction

In the eighth chapter of Matthew our Lord expresses His authority. Having preached a monumental sermon in chapters 5 through 7, He faces the inevitable questions: "What gives You the right to speak like that? Who do You think You are? Where did You come from? What is Your authority?" Chapters 8 and 9 supply the answers to those questions. In these two chapters Jesus says in effect that He is God. He demonstrates His supernatural power in a series of incredible miracles that could be explained in no other way than that God was present. Matthew continues his presentation of the kingship of Christ by giving us the credentials of the King.

Now let me give you a little background so that you can better understand the drama of this passage.

A. Disease in the Time of Christ

1. Explained

In the time of Christ disease was rampant throughout the world. Medical science was for all intents and purposes nonexistent, so disease could not be dealt with properly. Since disease was left to run its course, there were many sick and dying people. There was a tremendous fear of disease because of the pain and suffering that accompanied it. There were few drugs that could alleviate the pain. Diseases of epidemic proportions wiped out entire cities. It was common for people to die very young.

The Bible mentions many diseases that existed at the time of Christ and in Old Testament times. Here is an idea of the variety of diseases that the Lord would have confronted:

a) Atrophy

The term *atrophy* encompasses diseases like muscular dystrophy, a condition in which muscles refuse to absorb nutrients and consequently become thinner and weaker. It also includes poliomyelitis, a disease brought by a virus in the bowel that attacks the central nervous system.

22

b) Blindness

Blindness was rampant at the time of Christ. It came about very commonly at the birth of one whose mother was infected with gonorrhea. Blindness also resulted from trachoma, unsanitary conditions, brilliant sunlight, intense heat, blowing sand, or war.

c) Boils/Tumors

Boils include carbuncles, abscesses, and infected glands.

d) Deafness

Deafness could be caused by a birth defect, a wound or injury, or an infected middle or inner ear.

e) Dropsy

Dropsy, or edema, is symptomized by a retention of body fluids.

f) Dumbness

Dumbness, or mutism, is the inability to speak.

g) Dysentery

Dysentery is caused by amebae, bacteria, or worms and affects the colon and the digestive tract.

h) Epilepsy

Epilepsy is typically manifested by petit mal (small) or grand mal (great) seizures.

i) Hemorrhaging

Bleeding can be caused by fibroid tumors that are often cancerous.

j) Speech impediments

Speech impediments include various types of aphasia, a complete or partial inability to speak.

k) Indigestion/ulcers

Indigestion could involve severe stomach disorders.

l) Inflammation

Inflammation or swelling often come as a result of infections caused by strep and staph bacteria.

m) Pestilence

Pestilence could refer to any infectious disease of epidemic proportions.

n) Skin disease/leprosy

o) Paralysis

p) Fever

All of those diseases existed in Jesus' time in their various forms and were for the most part unable to be alleviated. Because there was no effective way of dealing with those diseases, people became very aware of the doom that hung over their heads.

2. Eliminated

However, Jesus touched human life at the point of its greatest agony—disease. In fact, Jesus virtually wiped out sickness in Palestine during His earthly ministry. The monumental nature of His work is beyond description. We can't fully appreciate it, because we live in a society that can manage disease fairly well. Although there are some cures that are elusive, such as the cure for cancer or heart disease, we have eliminated many diseases and even have the capacity to alleviate pain. But in Jesus' time, there was no such comfort. Consequently, as He swept through Palestine with His healing power affecting many thousands of people, His miraculous power became a staggering revelation that He was God. Repeatedly He made statements like, "Believe me for the very works' sake" (John 14:11). There was no way one could rationally deny the all-encompassing, widespread healings that He had done.

a) Matthew 12:15—"But when Jesus knew [about the conspiracy of the Pharisees to kill Him], he withdrew himself from there; and great multitudes followed him and he healed them all."

b) Matthew 14:14—"And Jesus went forth, and saw a great multitude, and was moved with compassion toward them, and he healed their sick." Jesus healed all who came to Him and, in so doing, practically banished disease from Palestine.

B. Disbelief in the Miracles of Christ

Never in the history of the world did so many healings take place. Only a divine explanation was possible. That is what makes the Pharisees' unbelief so utterly incredible. It shows the depth of the sin in their hearts. They would not believe Christ in spite of such humanly inexplicable evidence. For that reason, Matthew indirectly indicts them as he points out the credentials of Jesus as Messiah by recording three of the healings He performed.

Review

I. THE WRETCHED MAN (vv. 1-4; see pp. 10-18)

Jesus reached to the very lowest levels of society. That was an indirect condemnation of the pride of the Pharisees, who never would have stooped beneath their pious dignity. He showed that the extent of His kingdom went beyond the high and the mighty by reaching out to people whom nobody else would touch. His kingdom was not what most expected; it was not for the super pious, but for the desperate and the hurting. So Christ touched a man with leprosy and healed him.

Lesson

II. THE RESPECTED MAN (vv. 5-13)

In this passage, we find a man who was considered an outcast by the Jewish people because he was a Gentile. Worse than that, he was a Roman soldier, a member of the occupying army that had invaded their precious land. Although he was despised as much as a leper, the Lord healed his servant. By so doing, He reinforced the fact that His kingdom included the outcast and the Gentile. Its parameters were far broader than the Pharisees had assumed.

A. The Place (v. 5a)

"And when Jesus was entered into Capernaum."

Some commentators think that all three of the miracles recorded in chapter eight happened the same day after Jesus had finished the Sermon on the Mount, come down from the mountain, and entered Capernaum, a town on the northwest shore of the Sea of Galilee. Ironically, although it is one of the most beautiful places I've ever seen, the ancient town doesn't exist anymore, because Jesus pronounced a curse on it. Jesus resided there while ministering in Galilee, staying perhaps at the house of Peter.

B. The Person (v. 5b)

"There came unto him a centurion, beseeching him."

Matthew records the basic conversation of the centurion and Jesus, but the comparative passage in Luke 7 elucidates some of the details. Luke tells us that the centurion didn't actually go to Jesus himself, but sent some Jewish elders with his message because he felt unworthy to have Christ in his home.

1. A centurion

Every time a centurion appears in the New Testament, he is seen in a very positive light. It's as if the Lord purposely picked out some of the most hated people in Palestine to illustrate the extent of His grace in reaching beyond Israel to establish His kingdom. The redemption of such individuals is a slap in the face to Jewish exclusivism, which had no room for a Gentile, especially a Roman solider.

2. A Samaritan

If it was bad to be a Gentile from a Jewish perspective, it was worse to be a Roman soldier. The Roman occupying army was trained in the communities of Palestine, enlisting non-Jewish people from the areas it was occupying. The centurion in Matthew 8 would have been a solider over the troops of Antipas, and it is likely that he was a Samaritan. The worst kind of Gentile in Jewish eyes was a Samaritan, because Samaritans were descendants of Jews who had intermarried with Gentiles, thereby forfeiting their Jewish heritage.

25

So here was the worst kind of Gentile—a Samaritan. He was also the worst kind of Samaritan—a member of the occupying forces of Rome. Any Pharisee would say, "Why would anyone ever do a favor for somebody like that?" That is precisely the point Jesus wanted to make. The Pharisees had an incorrect view on the parameters of the kingdom. They believed that it was confined to them, having an "us-four-no-more-shut-the-door" mentality. Consequently, when Jesus threw the door to the kingdom wide open, that was more than they could accept, and their hatred of Him grew until they finally killed Him.

C. The Petition (vv. 6-9)

1. His respect (v. 6)

"[He said] Lord, my servant [Gk., *pais;* lit., "child"] lieth at home sick of the palsy [Gk., *paralutikos,* "paralysis"], grievously tormented."

The centurion addressed Jesus as "Lord," recognizing His divine authority as many other centurions did. He petitioned Jesus on behalf of a child. Luke, using the word *doulos,* which means "bondslave," recorded that the child was actually one of the centurion's slaves. It was rather common to have a child slave in the house. So we see that the centurion not only had respect for the Lord, but also for his boy slave, who was in tremendous pain at his home and possibly paralyzed with some disorder of the nervous system.

There is something beautiful about the centurion's petition. It shows that he cared about a servant, and that set him apart from just about everybody else in the Roman world, because in the Roman Empire, slaves were of no consequence. If they suffered or died, few cared. For example, Aristotle said that there could be no friendship or justice toward inanimate things, indeed, not even toward a horse, an ox, or a slave, since master and slave had nothing in common. He said, "A slave is a living tool, and a tool is an inanimate slave" (*Ethics,* 1161b). Gaius, an expert on Roman law, said that it was universally accepted that the master possessed the power of life and death over a slave (*Institutes,* I:52). It was legally acceptable to kill your slave if you didn't like him. Varro, a Roman nobleman who wrote on agriculture, said, in effect, that the only difference between a slave, a beast, and a cart was that a slave could talk (*On Landed Estates,* 1:17.1). Cato the Elder, a Roman writer, gave advice to somebody taking over a farm. He recommended that he look over the livestock and hold a sale. Then he told him to sell worn-out oxen, blemished cattle, blemished sheep, wool, hides, an old wagon, old tools, an old slave, a sickly slave, and whatever else was superfluous (*On Agriculture,* 2,7). Although the Romans viewed a slave as a thing, this centurion was different. He wasn't asking Jesus for something on his own behalf, but for his paralyzed servant. What an excellent perspective!

2. His reputation

The centurion was able to find Jewish leaders to bring his message to Jesus. Most Jewish people would have refused to do the bidding of a centurion, but those leaders were willing to come to Jesus on his behalf. Luke 7 tells us that when the Jewish elders came to Jesus, "They besought him earnestly, saying that he was worthy for whom he should do this: For he loveth our nation, and he hath built us a synagogue" (vv. 4-5). Evidently understanding something of the truth in Judaism, that God-fearing Gentile realized that he was dealing with the covenant people of the living God and made an investment in them. I've been in Capernaum and have stood in the ruins of the synagogue there. People say that its foundation came from Christ's day and was possibly even purchased by that very centurion.

There is no doubt that those Jewish leaders knew Jesus could heal. But if they were typical of the other religious leaders in Palestine, their hardness of heart kept them from taking the recognition of His ability a step further and accepting Him as Messiah and Savior. The centurion, who had expressed his love for a slave by desiring his healing, was a humble man. He wouldn't come to Jesus himself because he didn't feel worthy. He didn't want Jesus to have to enter his house, because he knew that a Jew was forbidden to enter the house of a Gentile. Rather than violating that tradition, the centurion chose to honor it. He didn't even ask Jesus to heal his servant; he merely informed Him of the situation.

3. His reward (v. 7)

"And Jesus saith unto him, I will come and heal him."

Jesus told the messengers sent by the centurion that He would come to the Gentile's home to heal the boy. But, according to Luke, Jesus never arrived. Realizing that Christ was coming, the centurion panicked because he didn't feel worthy to be in His presence and didn't want Him to have to violate Jewish law by coming in his house.

4. His response (vv. 8-9)

a) Of humility (v. 8*a*)

"The centurion answered and said, Lord, I am not worthy that thou shouldest come under my roof."

His message expressed his humility: "Lord, don't come any farther—I'm not worthy for You to enter my house. I can't allow You to come into my presence." There are some people who think they do God a favor by becoming a Christian. The truth is that we are not even worthy to enter His presence. I love the centurion's response!

That unique man had to work his way up through the ranks in the Roman army. He had to be tough because he led a hundred men. However, even though he was a combat-oriented drill sergeant, he was clearly a gentle, humble, meek, sensitive, and loving man who even cared for a sick slave. He was a true God-fearing Gentile like Cornelius in Acts 10.

b) Of faith (vv. 8*b*-9)

(1) His knowledge of Jesus' ability (v. 8*b*)

"But speak the word only, and my servant shall be healed."

You say, "Where did he get that information?" He had been around and had seen what Jesus was doing. Because he knew that Jesus could heal from a distance by just speaking a word, I believe he sensed that to stand before Jesus was to be in the presence of God.

(2) His knowledge of Jesus' authority (v. 9)

"For I am a man under authority, having soldiers under me; and I say to this man, Go, and he goeth; and to another, Come, and he cometh; and to my servant, Do this, and he doeth it."

The centurion was saying, "I understand Your authority There might be some around here who would question it, but I know a man with authority when I see one. I've seen what You've done and I know the power of Your words." He reasoned from the lesser to the greater. In effect, he said, "I am under authority and I can command things to happen. But You are above all authorities—how much more can You but speak a word and cause anything to happen!" That is great faith.

D. The Praise (v. 10)

1. Jesus' recognition (v. 10*a*)

"When Jesus heard it, he marveled."

You have got to have a unique kind of faith to amaze Jesus, because He knows everything. So when the text says that Jesus marveled, you know that is quite a statement. It tells us that Jesus in His humanness was literally amazed at the faith of that Gentile. His great faith was a taste of things to come, because there have been countless other Gentiles who have had that kind of faith in Christ.

2. Jesus' rebuke (v. 10*b*)

"[Jesus] said to them that followed, Verily I say unto you, I have not found so great faith, no, not in Israel."

The implication is that He should have found such faith among the people of the covenant promises and inheritance. He had found a certain amount among the Jewish people but never with that much virtue. The centurion's unique response showed his love, thoughtfulness, humility, sensitivity, and absolute confidence in the power and deity of Christ. Even Christ's own disciples on occasion had to be rebuked by Jesus for their "little faith" (Matt. 6:30; 8:26; 14:31; 16:8). They weren't even too sure who He was during His earthly ministry. When Philip asked Jesus to show them the Father, Jesus replied, "Have I been such a long time with you, and yet hast thou not known me, Philip?" (John 14:9). Even after others had testified of Jesus' resurrection, Thomas wouldn't believe until he saw Christ himself. But the centurion had great faith. His example shows that some Gentiles would demonstrate greater faith than some Jewish people. Isn't that true today? The church predominately is a Gentile church; Israel still rejects Jesus as her Messiah. Jesus went on to make that clear in one of His most devastating statements.

E. The Prediction (vv. 11-12)

1. The inclusion of Gentiles in the kingdom (v. 11)

"And I say unto you that many shall come from the east and west, and shall sit down with Abraham, and Isaac, and Jacob, in the kingdom of heaven."

a) Described

There is coming a great and glorious kingdom called the millennial kingdom, and it will be followed by an eternal kingdom. In that first kingdom, God's wonderful promise to Abraham, Isaac, and Jacob will come to pass. God brought the covenant through them, therefore, there is an essential Jewishness in the future of God's plans for the world. Salvation comes through Abraham's seed, and we are sons of Abraham by faith, so we receive blessing because we are part of that same covenant. That is precisely what Jesus was saying in verse 11. The many who would come from the East and the West are those from the Gentile world, which is literally to the east and west of Israel. Jesus predicted that His kingdom would be filled with Gentiles.

b) Denied

Most Jewish people didn't believe that, however. Such a shocking statement was contrary to their tradition. They believed that all the Gentiles would be destroyed before the kingdom came. If you read some apocryphal literature like 2 Baruch 29, you would find that it pictures a great feast where all the Jews will sit down with the Messiah and eat behemoth and leviathan (designations of the largest land and sea animals.) Never for a moment did the Jews believe that the Gentiles would be reclining with them at the messianic banquet. But two thousand years later here we are, a church filled with Gentiles, and we will sit down someday in the millennial kingdom with Abraham, Isaac, and Jacob.

Now, if that isn't devastating enough, note what verse 12 says.

2. The exclusion of Jews from the kingdom (v. 12)

a) The promise to the Jews (v. 12*a*)

"But the sons of the kingdom shall be cast out into outer darkness; there shall be weeping and gnashing of teeth."

That is a very powerful statement. The Jewish people were called "sons of the kingdom," because by right they are the heirs of the promises and privileges that were given to them (cf. Ps. 147:19-20; Isa. 63:8-9; Rom. 9:4; Eph. 2:12). In spite of that, many will not be part of the kingdom, because one doesn't enter it on the basis of physical lineage. In John 8, the Jewish rulers boast that they are the sons of Abraham. Jesus said, "I know that ye are Abraham's seed; but ye seek to kill me, because my word hath no place in you. I speak that which I have seen with my Father, and ye do that which ye have seen with your father. They answered, and said unto him, Abraham is our father. Jesus saith unto them, If ye were Abraham's children, ye would do the works of Abraham. But now ye seek to kill me. . . . Ye are of your father the devil" (vv. 37-40*a*, 44*a*). They hated Him for saying that. Proudly assuming their right to enter, many sons of the kingdom are going to be thrown out, having forfeited their inheritance by unbelief.

b) The punishment of the Jews (v. 12*b*)

(1) The place

"Outer darkness" was a meaningful phrase in Jewish thought. The rabbis taught that sinners in Gehenna would be covered with darkness. They believed that sinners would be sent away from the light of God's presence. Paradoxically, hell is not only a place of darkness; it is also a place of fire. Its supernatural quality enables fire to exist in total darkness, a phenomenon created by God for eternal punishment. Outer darkness is a place, just like heaven.

(2) The pain

The horrible result of that punishment will be "weeping and gnashing of teeth." The darkness will cause a loss of all happiness. It will produce helpless despair and endless torment in eternal blackness.

(*a*) Matthew 13:42—"And shall cast them into a furnace of fire; there shall be wailing and gnashing of teeth" (cf. v. 50).

(*b*) Matthew 22:13—"Then said the king to the servants, Bind him hand and foot, and take him away, and cast him into outer darkness; there shall be weeping and gnashing of teeth."

(*c*) Matthew 24:51—"And shall cut him asunder, and appoint him his portion with the hypocrites; there shall be weeping and gnashing of teeth."

30

Although some people think that Jesus just talked about love, the gospels make it clear that He talked a lot about hell. I have been criticized for being too confrontive. But I have never preached a sermon as strong as Jesus did. I have never said anything as devastating as what He said. The message of Jesus is that people who reject Him as the Messiah—even if they are sons of the kingdom—are going to be thrown into outer darkness. So Jesus gave a sermon in the midst of healing the centurion's servant that was not easy to forget.

F. The Promise (v. 13)

"And Jesus said unto the centurion, Go thy way; and as thou hast believed, so be it done unto thee. And his servant was healed in the very same hour."

Jesus said, "You can all go back home—he's healed." Can you imagine the little servant boy popping out of his bed and saying, "I don't know what you did, sir, but I'm healed"? And can you imagine how much greater the centurion's faith was after his servant had been healed?

Notice the phrase "as thou hast believed, so be it done unto thee." Can we claim that? Not necessarily. Jesus said that to the centurion. Paul believed that God could heal him, but He didn't. That was His sovereign choice. Sometimes God heals people who have no faith. In fact, the Bible doesn't say that the little boy had any faith at all. Jesus healed him for the benefit of the centurion and everybody else in history who would read about him. As a result, I think there's one more centurion in heaven, and probably one more little boy as well.

Do you see what Jesus was saying here? "I reach for lepers and outcast Gentiles because My kingdom encompasses those who believe in Me, not those who are of some particular race." Now just in case his Jewish readers might completely come apart at the seams, Matthew adds one more healing in the next two verses.

III. THE RELATIVE (vv. 14-15)

A. The Situation (v. 14a)

Mark and Luke tell us that He entered the home during the Sabbath (Mark 1:29; Luke 4:38). Jesus had been at the synagogue. As Jesus, James, and John came in the door, possibly to share a meal, they found Peter's mother-in-law sick with a fever. The disciples asked Christ to heal her. From this account, we know that Peter was married. We find other evidence in 1 Corinthians 9:5, where Paul says that it was not wrong for Peter (Cephas) to allow his wife to travel with him in his ministry.

When the Pharisees got up in the morning, they were known to say, "I thank Thee that I am not a slave, a Gentile, or a woman." They believed that such people were at the bottom of society. Because of their low view of women, Jesus' healing of Peter's mother-in-law was another cause for an indictment against Him. He was clearly showing His disapproval of their tradition.

B. The Sickness (v. 15a)

"And he touched her hand, and the fever left her."

The hypothalamus in the middle of the brain controls a person's body temperature, keeping it at 98.6 degrees. However, infection in other parts of the body can overwhelm it. As the body attempts to fight the infection, its temperature can rise to as high as 108 degrees.

We don't know whether her fever was the result of malaria or some other disease, but Luke indicates that it was so severe, she could have died from it (Luke 4:38). However, Jesus reached out His hand and touched her. Immediately the fever left her.

C. The Service (v. 15b)

"And she arose, and ministered unto him."

In gratitude for being healed, Peter's mother-in-law prepared a meal for Jesus and the others.

I believe the miraculous healing of Peter's mother-in-law was included because she was Jewish. It would have been hard for a Jewish person to accept the healing of a leper and a Gentile and hear Jesus say that many were going to be shut out of the kingdom. So Matthew records Jesus' healing of a Jewish woman, almost as if to say, "Yes, the kingdom will embrace Gentiles, but I'll never turn My people Israel aside." There will be healing for them too. In Romans, Paul says that the Gentiles have been grafted onto a tree whose natural branches of unbelieving Jews have been cut off (11:17-24). But the day is coming when Israel will be grafted in again to the stock of blessing (11:24-25). I see that truth inherent in the healing of Peter's mother-in-law. If you can deny that Christ is God in the face of the healings He did, it is not because there is no evidence; it is because there is no faith in your heart.

Focusing on the Facts

1. What are some questions that Jesus would have been asked after He preached the sermon recorded in Matthew 5-7 (see p. 22)?

2. Identify some diseases of the time of Christ. Why were many of them a cause for fear (see pp. 22-23)?

3. What effect did Jesus' earthly ministry have upon disease in Palestine (see p. 24)?

4. Why would many Jewish leaders have criticized Jesus for doing a favor for a centurion (see p. 25)?

5. What did the centurion's petition show? Why was that unusual in the Roman world (see p. 26)?

6. How does Luke show us that the centurion was a God-fearing Gentile who

was held in high esteem (Luke 7:4-5; see p. 27)?

7. Although many Jewish leaders knew Jesus could heal, what were most not willing to recognize (see p. 27)?

8. How did the centurion demonstrate his humility (see p. 27)?

9. What two things did the centurion's faith demonstrate a knowledge of (see p. 28)?

10. What caused Jesus to be amazed (see p. 28)?

11. Where should Jesus have found faith like the centurion's? Why did Jesus occasionally have to rebuke His disciples (see p. 28)?

12. In what way is there an essential Jewishness to God's plans for the world (see p. 29)?

13. Who did Jesus predict would come from the East and the West and sit down with Abraham in the kingdom (see p. 29)?

14. According to their tradition, who did the Jewish people believe would be included in the kingdom (see p. 29)?

15. How will many Jewish people forfeit their inheritance (see p. 30)?

16. What is the paradoxical punishment that those who reject Jesus as Messiah will receive (see p. 30)?

17. Can we claim the same healing that Jesus promised to the centurion's servant? Explain (see p. 31).

18. How did the healing of Peter's mother-in-law show that Jesus disapproved of Jewish tradition (see p. 32)?

19. What is one possible reason Matthew records the healing of a Jew after saying that many Jewish people would be excluded from the kingdom? What type of healing is still in store for Israel (see p. 32)?

Pondering the Principles

1. The centurion was held in high esteem by many Jewish people in spite of the fact that he was a Roman soldier and possibly even a Samaritan. Do you think that those who disagree with your philosophy of life, or more specifically, your commitment to Christ, hold you in high esteem because of your personal integrity? Do you uphold the same high standards of godliness whether you are at work, at home, in the community, on vacation, or anywhere else? If you do, even those who would oppose you can have reason to respect you. Consider the early church as they preached a controversial message. The Jewish leaders had rejected and crucified their Messiah, who had risen from the dead. Among other things, Acts 2 characterizes the early church as having unity of mind, gladness, and sincerity of heart (v. 46; NASB). As a result, what were other people's response to them, according to verse 47? Then, even after the fear-inspiring discipline of Ananias and Sapphira, how did people feel toward the church according to Acts 5:13? Are you willing to uphold the smallest commands of God as much as the more important ones? Such integrity can have a dynamic impact upon the watching world.

2. Compare your faith to that of the centurion's. Do you think your faith would give Jesus any cause to marvel? Have you stretched your faith lately by believing God for something that is humanly impossible? Do you have reservations about Jesus' power or His authority? If so, meditate upon Matthew 28:18; John 11:38-44; 20:30-31; Colossians 1:15-20; Hebrews 1-2; and Revelation 5.

3
What Keeps Men from Christ?

Outline

Introduction
A. The Rejection of Christ
B. The Responses to Christ
C. The Revelation of Christ
   1. A compassionate preview
   2. A consummation of prophecy
      a) Spiritual healing
      b) Sympathetic feeling
         (1) Of the pain of sickness
         (2) Of the power of sin

Lesson
I. Personal Comfort
  A. The Change of Scene
  B. The Choice of a Scribe
    1. His office
    2. His offer
  C. The Challenge of the Savior
    1. Discerning the dedication
    2. Paying the price
      a) Matthew 10
      b) John 15-16
      c) 2 Timothy 3
      d) Matthew 5
      e) Hebrews 11
II. Personal Riches
  A. The Request of a Son
    1. His words
    2. His wait
  B. The Response of the Savior
    1. Explained
    2. Exemplified
      a) The request
      b) The response
      c) The regret

Introduction

A. The Rejection of Christ

What makes Christ refuse would-be followers? In some ways it is utterly incredible that people continually reject the lordship of Jesus Christ. It is almost beyond understanding that people reject Christ as the incomparable, gracious Son of God, the Savior of the world who died for them and still despise Him as much today as when He first came.

As you study the gospel of Matthew, it becomes very apparent that unbelieving people stubbornly refuse to accept all that Christ has done, for His credentials are obvious. The proof of His existence as God in human flesh is beyond contradiction. His words, works, death, and resurrection all speak unmistakably of the reality that Jesus is the Christ of God, the Savior of the world. In spite of that, Scripture records that people rejected the evidence and refused to acknowledge Christ as Lord. John 1:11 says, "He came unto his own, and his own received him not." Jesus says in John 5:40, "And ye will not come to me, that ye might have life." Shortly before His crucifixion, people cried out, "We will not have this man to reign over us" (Luke 19:14*b*). Those statements go against the affirmations that people made when they were confronted with His miracles.

B. The Responses to Christ

The world is like a judge in a court who has heard an open-and-shut case and made a verdict opposite the facts. For example, the people had witnessed the evidence of His

    1. Authority

    The words of Jesus were absolutely unique. Matthew 7:28-29 says, "The people were astonished at his doctrine; for he taught them as one having authority."

    2. Works

    The works of Jesus were undeniably divine. John 7:46 says, "Never man spoke like this man." The blind man in John 9 says this to his inquisitors: "Why here is a marvelous thing, that ye know not from where he is, and yet he hath opened mine eyes. . . . If this man were not of God, he could do nothing" (vv. 30, 33).

    3. Wisdom

    The wisdom of Jesus was superhuman. In Matthew 22, the Herodians (a political party that supported the rule of Rome) confronted Him with a coin and asked, "Is it lawful to give tribute unto Caesar, or not?'' (v. 17*b*). And Jesus said, "Render, therefore, unto Caesar the things which are Caesar's; and unto God, the things that are God's. When they heard these words, they marveled'' (vv. 21*b*-22*a*).

4. Purity

   His purity was undeniable. He challenged the Pharisees in John 8, saying, "Which of you convicteth me of sin?'' (v. 46*a*). The point is, they couldn't.

5. Truthfulness

   His truthfulness was beyond question. In John 8:46 He asked, "If I say the truth, why do ye not believe me?''

6. Power

   His power fascinated people. In Luke 8:25 the disciples said, "What manner of man is this! For He commandeth even the winds and water, and they obey him.''

7. Provision

   He miraculouly provided food for a multitude. In John 6:26, when they showed up again the next day, Jesus told them, "Ye seek me, not because ye saw the miracles, but because ye did eat of the loaves, and were filled.''

8. Healing

   He healed the sicknesses of many. Matthew 9:8 says, "But when the multitudes saw [the healing of the paralytic], they marveled, and glorified God, who had given such power unto men.''

9. Love

   His love was amazing. Those who stood at the grave of Lazarus said, "Behold how he loved him!'' when they saw Jesus weep (John 11:36).

10. Dominion over demons

    When Jesus cast a demon out in Matthew 9:33, "the multitudes marveled, saying, It was never so seen in Israel.''

11. Judgment

    His judgment was awesome. Jesus curses a fig tree, and it withers in Matthew 21:19. "And when the disciples saw it, they marveled'' (v. 20*a*).

12. Composure

    His composure was beyond that of others. He was silent before Pilate, who had power over His life. He showed no fear and gave no defense as Matthew 27:14 indicates: "He answered him never a word, insomuch that the governor marveled greatly.''

13. Teaching

    His teaching was far beyond any teacher that anyone had ever known. John 7:15 records that "the Jews marveled, saying, How knoweth this man letters, having never learned?'' When He was a boy of twelve, the teachers in the Temple "were amazed at his understanding and answers" (Luke 2:47).

14. Independence

His independence from the Jewish traditions made the religious leaders shudder. Luke 11:38 records that when Jesus accepted an invitation to eat with a Pharisee, His host "marveled that he had not first washed before dinner." He defied their meaningless ceremonies.

15. Tender condescension

His tender condescension shocked many. Jesus humbly conversed with a Samaritan harlot. John 4:27 says, "And upon this came his disciples, and marveled that he talked with the woman."

People clearly saw that everything about Jesus was astounding and humanly inexplicable. Is it any wonder, then, that in Mark 6:6, Jesus "marveled because of their unbelief"? How could people be exposed to such a vast number of convincing credentials and yet walk away? For some there is an overt, willful love of sin. John 3:19 says, "Men loved darkness rather than light, because their deeds were evil." People don't want to come to the light of righteousness because they love the darkness of sin, and the light will expose their sin. That is why they deny the evidence and run the other way. Some people are attracted to Jesus' charisma and power. They are the thrill seekers who want to get in on the action but don't want to make a commitment. The church has plenty of them. They may claim to be born again and to be following Jesus, but they're just as lost as the ones who turn and run from the light. In Matthew 8 we meet three such thrill seekers.

C. The Revelation of Christ

1. A compassionate preview (v. 16)

"When the evening was come, they brought unto him many that were possessed with demons; and he cast out the spirits with his word, and healed all that were sick."

As soon as the Sabbath had come to a close, people came to Jesus with the sick and the demon possessed, and He healed all of them. It was always that way. One didn't have to search very long to find a miracle, for Jesus performed thousands of them. Whether the diseases were spiritual, as in the case of demon possession, or physical, Jesus healed all those who came to Him regardless of their faith or circumstances. In so doing, He was giving evidence of His messiahship and deity. His acts of healing were part of His ongoing ministry. Matthew 12:15 says that "great multitudes followed him, and he healed them all." Matthew 14:14 says, "And Jesus went forth, and saw a great multitude, and was moved with compassion toward them, and he healed their sick." He virtually banished disease from Palestine.

38

If someone marched through the countryside healing people, he probably would attract a crowd. Even phony healers today can draw crowds. And people who go away from them as sick as they were when they showed up often insist on trying to find another healer. So when a true healer appeared, the crowd became larger and larger.

Now why did Jesus heal so many people? If we said it was because of His compassion, we would be right. He had compassion on people, despising disease and death because He knew they were the result of sin reigning in the world. Furthermore, Jesus healed people because He was giving them a preview of His kingdom. Do you know what will happen when Christ sets up His eternal kingdom? There will be no more death, sorrow, pain, or sickness (Rev. 21:4).

But there is another reason Jesus healed people.

2. A consummation of prophecy (v. 17)

"That it might be fulfilled which was spoken by Isaiah, the prophet, saying, he himself took our infirmities, and bore our sicknesses."

The Old Testament had predicted many things about the Messiah of God, the Savior of the world, who, as the Lamb of God, would take away sin. Jesus showed Himself to be the very fulfillment of those prophecies. Among the many prophecies, Isaiah 53:4-5 states that the Messiah would bear our griefs and sorrows and bring healing. In His earthly ministry, Jesus wonderfully dealt with disease and sickness, giving the people a taste of what His kingdom would be like—free from all sickness, death, and sin.

a) Spiritual healing

Matthew 8:17, which says, "He himself took our infirmities, and bore our sicknesses," is taken from Isaiah 53, a prediction of the substitutionary death of Christ. Important to our present understanding are verses 4-6: "Surely he hath borne our griefs, and carried our sorrows; yet we did esteem him stricken, smitten of God, and afflicted. But he was wounded for our transgressions, he was bruised for our iniquities; the chastisement for our peace was upon him, and with his stripes we are healed. All we like sheep have gone astray; we have turned every one to his own way, and the Lord hath laid on him the iniquity of us all." This great prophecy tells us that Jesus died for our sins. When Isaiah said, "with his stripes we are healed," he was not referring specifically to physical healing. Rather, he was referring to the spiritual healing of the disease of sin. However, when sin is healed, sickness is indirectly healed as well, because sickness is a result of sin.

Some people ask, "Isn't there physical healing in the atonement?" The answer is yes, there is, but it isn't for now—it's for later. When Jesus died on the cross, did He take away our sin? Yes. Do you as a Christian still have trouble with sin? Yes. Jesus dealt with our sin, but the fulfillment of that is yet future in the fullest sense. When He died on the cross, did He destroy the enemy death? Yes. But do Christians die? Yes. the fulfillment of that is yet future. When He died on the cross, did He deal with disease? Yes. Do we still get sick? Yes. That also is to be completed in the future. Yes, there's healing in the atonement, just as there's deliverance from death and a full restoration of the believer before God in the atonement—but still we wait for that day. People who say that Christians should never be sick because there's healing in the atonement are forced to logically conclude that a Christian should never sin or die. It is no more correct to teach that Christians should be free from illness that to say that a Christian should be free from sin or death.

Christ died primarily for our sins, not our sicknesses. The gospel is good news about forgiveness, not health (Acts 26:18). Christ was made sin, not disease (2 Cor. 5:21), and Christ took away our sin, not our sickness (John 1:29). We should never interpret Isaiah 53 any differently than to say that it primarily means Jesus came and died to heal us from sin. First Peter 2:24 reinforces the fact that the cross was designed primarily to heal sin: "Who his own self bore our sins in his own body on the tree, that we, being dead to sins, should live unto righteousness; by whose stripes ye were healed." Peter is talking about a spiritual healing from sin. But Matthew adds the physical dimension. He opens up to us the fact that Isaiah 53:4 extends from the sin problem to sickness.

Yes, there's healing and wholeness in the atonement, but only as it comes to us in the fullness of salvation, when our bodies are glorified in His eternal kingdom. Someday He will take away all our sicknesses. But the healing that took place during His earthly ministry was only a foretaste of that which was spoken by the prophet Isaiah.

b) Sympathetic feeling

(1) Of the pain of sickness

Jesus also bore our sicknesses in that He sympathetically felt pain. Being omniscient, Christ knew what was in the heart of man; He could read the mind. In John 3, Nicodemus comes to Jesus and without even asking the question he has in his head, Jesus is able to give him an answer. He "knew what was in man" (John 2:25). Therefore, because He is omniscient, knowing everything you've ever felt, thought, or experienced, He can fully understand every pain you feel. That is why Hebrews 4:15 says that He is a sympathetic High Priest, who is "touched with the feeling of our infirmities." I believe He has borne our sicknesses in that He sympathetically feels the pain we feel. When Jesus saw the crowds, "he was moved with compassion" (Matt. 9:36). The word "compassion" literally means "to suffer with." Jesus didn't contract our diseases, but He fully felt our pain.

(2) Of the power of sin

When Christ bore our infirmities, He suffered from their root, the power of sin. For example, as He stood at the grave of Lazarus, who had been dead for a few days, the Bible says that He "groaned in the spirit" (John 11:33). The passage also says that He wept. What was He groaning and weeping about? It wasn't just because Lazarus was dead, for He was about to call him out of the grave. He was groaning and weeping because whenever He saw sickness, He anticipated the bitter reality of Calvary. He knew that the evil of sin caused all pain and sorrow. Living His life in the shadow of the cross, He never saw sickness without feeling the pain of sin.

Supremely, Jesus bore our sicknesses when He went to the cross. He dealt with sin in a devastating way, guaranteeing that disease would ultimately be destroyed. His healings were simply a preview of that marvelous day.

Although there were many Pharisees who hated Jesus because they "loved darkness rather than light" (John 3:19), there were others who were attracted to the magnetism of His personality. These were the thrill seekers. In each case, something kept them from genuine conversion.

Lesson

I. PERSONAL COMFORT (vv. 18-20)

A. The Change of Scene (v. 18)

"Now, when Jesus saw great multitudes about him, he gave commandment to depart unto the other side."

Jesus and His disciples had been on the western shore of the Sea of Galilee. Since the crowd around them was becoming so massive and the Lord was physically exhausted, they entered a boat to depart to the opposite shore. That gave the Lord some necessary time for prayer, meditation, and respite from the pressure of the crowds. Such pressures, not necessarily part of God's plan, motivated Jesus to leave for ministry in a new place.

By that time, many people were following Him. In fact, Mark tells us that several other boats followed behind Him like a little flotilla. So some people were at the very crux of decision: "Do I get in the boat and go, or do I stay?" Treating this event out of chronological order, Matthew presents his readers with two individuals who must make

41

similar decisions. In a parallel passage, Luke introduces us to a third person.

B. The Choice of a Scribe (v. 19)

"And a certain scribe came, and said unto him, Master, I will follow thee wherever thou goest."

The first man appeared to be interested in following Jesus, but he never did follow or come to true salvation, because he wanted personal comfort more than he wanted Christ.

1. His office

This man was a scribe, an authority in the law, who had the official sanction of the Jewish authorities to teach. They were highly educated and were loyal to the system. Generally siding with the Pharisees, the scribes joined in their opposition to Christ. For those reasons, it was unusual for a scribe to want to follow Jesus.

2. His offer

The scribe approached Jesus, saying, "Master [Gk., *didaskalos,* "teacher, rabbi"], I will follow thee wherever thou goest." What a tremendous statement of dedication! Apparently, he was making a permanent commitment. I am sure the scribe thought that Jesus was the greatest teacher he had ever heard, and when he saw Christ's miracles, he concluded that they were from God. He was attracted to the unique and impressive person of Christ.

If that man showed up at a church today, most people would immediately sign him up. But Jesus wasn't so eager. He tested the scribe's true level of commitment:

C. The Challenge of the Savior (v. 20)

"And Jesus saith unto him, The foxes have holes, and the birds of the air have nests, but the Son of man hath no where to lay his head."

1. Discerning the dedication

That is a proverbial saying that simply means Jesus would not regularly experience the basic comforts of life that wild animals had. When John 7:53 and 8:1 say, "And every man went unto his own house. Jesus went unto the Mount of Olives," the implication seems to be that He didn't have His own house. Often He would spend the night at the Mount of Olives in prayer with the Father. Although the gospels tell us that Jesus occasionally stayed in a house in Bethany, He had few personal possessions. He had no guarantee of comfort to offer the scribe. Being able to read his mind, Jesus forced him to face the unpleasant reality of discomfort. Although the scribe was probably thinking, "Jesus, my life is full and rich; I'm already satisfied. I just want to add You to my life-style," Jesus refused to take advantage of His popularity.

In John 2, after Jesus had done many miracles in Jerusalem, "Many believed in his name. . . . But Jesus did not commit himself unto them, because he knew all men, and needed not that any should testify of man; for he knew what was in man" (vv. 23-25). That means He had no faith in their faith, because He knew they were only thrill seekers. In fact, He classified such people in the parable of the sower as seeds that immediately spring up but are soon scorched by the sun because they have no root (Matt. 13:5-6). There are people who want to jump on the Christian bandwagon, but as soon as the persecution starts and following Christ is not comfortable anymore, they want out.

The scribe was captivated by Christ. But Jesus knew that human nature is fickle and self-centered. He knew that it hungers for sensations: the crowd, the miracles, and the excitement. The commentator Lenski described the scribe's fascination with Jesus in this way: "He sees the soldiers on parade, the fine uniforms and the glittering arms, and is eager to join, forgetting the exhausting marches, the bloody battles, the graves, perhaps unmarked" (*The Interpretation of St. Matthew's Gospel* [Minneapolis: Augsburg, 1961, pp. 338-39]). His shallow eagerness is like a seed on stony ground that grows quickly but dies under the heat of persecution. Evidently that man never understood the basic elements of discipleship—self-denial and suffering. After Jesus tells the scribe what he can expect in verse 20, you will notice the next verse doesn't say anything about him. Do you know why? He probably wasn't around. He left in the white space between verses 20 and 21. The Lord put him under a spotlight, and he vanished.

Jesus is so unlike us. We sugarcoat the gospel message so everybody can get saved as easily as possible. But Jesus told it like it was and in doing so kept a lot of insincere people from following Him.

2. Paying the price

Jesus affirmed that He was "the Son of man," a messianic title that first appears in Daniel 7:13 and is used in the gospels eighty-eight times. The term "Son of God" speaks of Jesus' deity, whereas "Son of man" emphasizes His humiliation. He is saying, "In My humble estate, I don't even have the basic comforts of life that foxes and birds have. And if you're going to follow Me, you need to be willing to give them up as well." In fact, the New Testament makes it clear that persecution would accompany those who follow Christ and live righteously.

a) Matthew 10

"Behold, I send you forth as sheep in the midst of wolves. . . . But beware of men; for they will deliver you up to the councils, and they will scourge you in their synagogues, and ye shall be brought before governors and kings. . . . But when they deliver you up, be not anxious how or what ye shall speak; for it shall be given you in that same hour what ye shall speak. . . . And ye shall be hated of all men for my name's sake. . . . But when they persecute you in this city, flee into another'' (vv. 16*a*, 17-18*a*, 19, 22*a*, 23*a*).

b) John 15-16

"The servant is not greater than his lord. If they have persecuted me, they will also persecute you" (15:20*b*). "These things have I spoken unto you, that ye should not be offended. They shall put you out of the synagogues; yea, the time cometh, that whosoever killeth you will think that he doeth God service. . . . In the world ye shall have tribulation" (16:1-2; 33*b*).

c) 2 Timothy 3

"Yea, and all that will live godly in Christ Jesus shall suffer persecution" (v. 12).

d) Matthew 5

"Blessed are ye, when men shall revile you, and persecute you, and shall say all manner of evil against you falsely, for my sake" (v. 11).

e) Hebrews 11

Many heroes of the faith "of whom the world was not worthy" were tortured and killed (v. 38).

There is a price to pay for being a Christian, but the scribe wasn't willing to pay it; he just wanted to add excitement to his life. He was a potential Judas, and nobody needs more of that type. So Jesus' explanation of the way things really are drove him away. If a young man expresses a desire for a scholarship, a school might ask him, "Are you prepared to scorn the delights of the world and study diligently in order to attain your goal?" When an explorer wants to gather a team to explore some uncharted portion of the earth, many may want to join him for the adventure until he tells them about the snow and ice, the searing heat, the swamps, and the wild animals. When a young person wants to be a great athlete, the good trainer asks him, "Are you willing to make the sacrifice that it takes to be great?" We do Jesus a grave disservice if we lead people to believe that the Christian way is an easy way. It is not. There is no thrill like following Christ, and there's no glory like the end of a life of obedience to Him, but Jesus never said it would be easy—He always said you had to take up your cross. People who want personal comfort plus Christ merely want to add Jesus to their previously established pattern of life. He refuses such people as His disciples.

There is a second person in Matthew 8 who didn't obtain entrance into the kingdom.

II. PERSONAL RICHES (vv. 21-22)

A. The Request of a Son (v. 21)

"And another of his disciples [followers] said unto him, Lord, permit me first to go and bury my father."

1. His words

That sounds like a reasonable request, doesn't it? A son couldn't just forget about his father if he were dead; he would have to bury him quickly, because Jewish people didn't embalm. Furthermore, Jewish custom taught that a person needed to mourn for his father and mother for thirty days after they had died. Genesis tells us that a son's final act of devotion to his parents was to make sure that he cared for their burial (25:9; 35:29; 49:28-33; 50:13-14). So maybe he was talking about needing a month to mourn and take care of family business. He knew the Lord was on the move in His ministry so he said, "I can't come know, but I'll try to catch up with You later after I bury my father." But there's a lot more here than meets the eye.

2. His wait

The son's request was a colloquial phrase that appears in the Middle East even in contemporary times. A missionary in the Middle East was talking with a rich young Turk, advising him to go on a tour of Europe upon completing his education. When the Turk replied that he must first bury his father, the missionary expressed his sympathy that the young man's father had died. But the Turk explained that his father was very much alive. He merely meant that he had to stay at home to fulfill his responsibility to his parents until his father died before he could go on the suggested tour.

The implication of the phrase "to bury one's father" can mean that a person would prefer to wait until his father passes away so that he can receive his inheritance. That seems to be what the son in Matthew 8 had in mind. In his indecision about whether to follow or not, he might have been thinking, "When I get my inheritance, think of how I can be used in the movement." The distraction of money took the courage and commitment out of his discipleship.

B. The Response of the Savior (v. 22)

"But Jesus said unto him, Follow me, and let the dead bury their dead."

1. Explained

At first, that sharp statement almost seems to be nonsensical; How can dead people bury other dead people? The solution must be that the first kind of dead people refer to those who are spiritually dead. To this proverbial statement Luke adds in the parallel passage, "But go thou and preach the kindgom of God" (9:60). In other words, Jesus is saying, "Let the spiritually dead bury the physically dead—let the secular world take care of its own issues—you have been called to the kingdom of God. You are functioning on the wrong level. Let the system take care of itself."

Jesus was not saying that Christians are forbidden to go to funerals or make sure that their father or mother get buried. He simply pointed out that the world's passing affairs are part of a dead system.

The young man's priorities were fouled up. He had stressed secular matters above spiritual ones. As a result, he left somewhere between verses 22 and 23. Personal possessions were important to him; he had waited a long time for his inheritance, and he wasn't going to leave now. He was attracted to Jesus by the thrill of the cause, but exhibited no commitment. He wanted his money more than he wanted the Messiah. He reminds me of the rich young ruler in Matthew 19.

2. Exemplified

   a) The request

     Verse 16 says, "And behold, one came and said unto him, Good Master, what good thing shall I do, that I may have eternal life?"

   b) The response

     Verse 21 says, "Jesus said unto him, If thou wilt be perfect, go and sell what thou hast, and give to the poor, and thou shalt have treasure in heaven; and come and follow me."

     No one gets saved by selling all his possessions and giving the money to the poor, but if money stands in the way of a man's relationship to God, he will have to get past it if he's going to be saved. Money distracts many people. It can prevent them from being committed to Christ and therefore entering His kingdom. Although the rich young ruler claimed he had kept all the law, Jesus knew that there was yet an obstacle that stood between him and his faith—money.

   c) The regret

     Verse 22 tells us, "But when the young man heard that saying, he went away sorrowful; for he had great possessions." He was sorry he couldn't get in the kingdom without holding onto his money. How foolish! But many people are like that. How sad it is that personal comfort and personal riches keep people from coming to Christ. They may be initially attracted to Him, but when they discover the price of commitment, they walk away—lost forever.

A third would-be-disciple came that day. Although Matthew doesn't tell us about him, Luke does.

III. PERSONAL RELATIONS

Luke 9 says, "And another also said, Lord, I will follow thee; but let me first go bid them farewell, who are at home at my house. And Jesus said unto him, No man, having put his hand to the plough, and looking back, is fit for the kingdom of God" (vv. 61-62).

A. The Pull of Parents

Jesus cited a popular proverb of His day, attributed to the Greek poet Hesiod from 800 B.C. It was: You can't plough a straight furrow when looking backward. That illustrates the need for a full commitment to one's goals. Jesus knew that the young man was more attached to his parents than he would be to Him. It wasn't his wife and kids he wanted to bid farewell to—it was his mommy and daddy. He was still dependent upon the influence of his parents. Jesus knew that intimidating emotional pleas and threats of being ostracized would keep that man from following Him as a disciple.

There are a lot of people like that. They would come to Christ, but they're afraid of what their families might say or do. Not wanting to be alienated, they stay in a false religious system, or they keep from following Christ out of fear. Such people are trying to plough a furrow while looking backwards.

B. The Parallel About Priorities

Matthew 10:34-37 says, "Think not that I am come to send peace on earth; I came not to send peace, but a sword. For I am come to set a man at variance against his father, and the daughter against her mother, and the daughter-in-law against her mother-in-law. And a man's foes shall be they of his own household. He that loveth father or mother more than me, is not worthy of me; and he that loveth son or daughter more than me, is not worthy of me." If devotion to one's parents holds a person back from full commitment to Christ, then he is not fit to enter the kingdom of God. Those verses are not talking about entering Christian service; they are talking about salvation. You can't get saved with priorities that demand more devotion than Christ. Jesus offered nothing to the young man who refused to commit his whole heart to Him. There is no such thing as halfhearted discipleship.

Conclusion

Personal relations, personal riches, and personal comfort all stand in the way of following Christ. Even though Jesus says in John 6:37 that "him that cometh to me I will in no wise cast out," He will not accept those who have no intention of making a true commitment. Such insincerity usually becomes evident when the demands become too great. That was the case later in the chapter when Jesus said, "Except ye eat the flesh of the Son of man, and drink his blood, ye have no life in you" (v. 53). What did He mean by that? You either take all, or you get nothing. After Jesus had made other challenging statements, many would-be disciples lost interest in following Him: "From that time many of his disciples went back, and walked no more with him" (v. 66). They weren't willing to make a full commitment, so He turned them down. Therefore, the verse needs to be qualified for our understanding. Jesus will not reject the person who comes to Him if he comes with a Beatitude attitude—begging in his spirit, mourning over his sin, meek before God, hungering and thirsting for righteousness, crying for mercy, and willing to be persecuted, hated, and reviled for His sake.

Focusing on the Facts

1. In spite of the fact that Jesus' words, works, death, and resurrection identify Him as the Christ of God, how did many people respond to Him (see p. 36)?

2. What seemed to be the overall response to the different elements of Christ's life (see pp. 36-38)?

3. How is it possible that people could be exposed to such a vast number of convincing credentials and yet respond the way that most did (see p. 38)?

4. Give two reasons Jesus healed people (see pp. 38-39).

5. How is the healing in Isaiah 53 primarily to be understood (see pp. 39-40)?

6. In what sense is there physical healing in the atonement? Why is it inconsistent to teach that Christians should never get sick (see pp. 39-40)?

7. As our sympathetic High Priest, what can Jesus feel on our behalf (Heb. 4:15; see p. 41)?

8. Knowing that He could raise Lazarus from the dead, why might Jesus have groaned "in his spirit" (see p. 41)?

9. When Jesus went to the cross and dealt with sin in such a devastating way, what was guaranteed with regard to disease (see p. 41)?

10. Why might Jesus have wanted to depart from the multitudes to the other side of the Sea of Galilee (see p. 41)?

11. What did the scribe apparently want more than following Jesus (see p. 42)?

12. Why was it unusual for a scribe to want to follow Jesus (see p. 42)?

13. According to Jesus' proverbial statement, who or what had more creature comforts than He did (see p. 42)?

14. Why didn't Jesus put His confidence in the faith of those who seemed eager to follow Him (John 2:23-25; see p. 43)?

15. In the parable of the sower, to what type of soil could the scribe be compared (see p. 43)?

16. How can we assume the scribe responded to Jesus? Why (see p. 43)?

17. Beside the humiliation of having no comfort, what does the New Testament say will accompany those who would follow Jesus in righteous living (see pp. 43-44)?

18. Although the son's request to bury his father sounded reasonable, what could have been his true intention, taken in the context of Jesus' response (see p. 45)?

19. Explain the meaning of Jesus' response to the son, "Let the dead bury their dead; but go thou and preach the kingdom of God" (Luke 9:60). In what way were the young man's priorities out of order (see pp. 45-46)?

20. How can money prevent a person from being saved (see p. 46)?

21. When is a person not fit for the kingdom of God, according to Luke 9:61-62? Why (see pp. 46-47)?

Pondering the Principles

1. If you have been miraculously healed by Jesus, or have a close friend or relative who has, take a moment and renew your thankfulness to God. On the other hand, if you know someone who is suffering right now, pray that God would give grace in the midst of the difficulty and provide healing if He so desires it. Next, read and meditate upon Hebrews 4:14-16, praising God for Jesus, our great High Priest, who can sympathetically identify with us and provide "grace to help in time of need" (v. 16*b*). Also, read Revelation 21:1-7, praising God that someday physical suffering, sorrow, and death will be vanquished.

2. Modern society emphasizes leisure time, and there are probably many people who have no desire to work hard. However, there are many who are "workaholics" because of our society's fast pace. Even in Christian circles, there are those who would "burn themselves out for the Lord." It is great to be sacrificially committed to Christ but not by failing to provide financial and spiritual support for your family (Eph. 6:4; 1 Tim. 5:8) or at the expense of your health (Acts 14:5-6; 1 Tim. 5:23). Notice the example of Jesus, who in the midst of the exhausting work of His ministry would take take for spiritual, physical, and emotional refreshment (Matt. 8:18; Mark 6:31-32; Luke 6:12; John 18:1-2). As dedicated as you may be to your work and ministry, plan now to allow time for necessary rest and refreshment. If you are part of a family, discuss together some places to go and some things to do that can not only provide mutual enjoyment, but also a revitalized outlook on your daily responsibilities.

3. Read 2 Corinthians 13:5. Evaluate yourself honestly. Are you similar in any respects to the scribe who loved comfort, the son who wanted to wait for his inheritance, or the young man who was still tied to his former relationships? Do you sense that you are only following Jesus at a distance or actually postponing a full commitment to Him as you focus your attention on some lesser priority? If you were to sit down with Jesus in a conversation and talk about the direction your discipleship is heading, what do you think He would say? Meditate upon Philippians 3:7-14. Commit the changes you need to make into God's care. To help ensure your commitment, get involved in a small group that can hold you accountable for your goals.

4
Jesus' Power over the Natural

Outline

Introduction
A. The Fall into Sin
B. The Future of Salvation
C. The Futility of Society
D. The Force of the Supernatural
   1. God's power recited in Scripture
     a) Psalm 62:11
     b) Job 26:14
     c) Psalm 79:11
     d) Nahum 1:3
     e) Isaiah 26:4
     f) Psalm 65:6
     g) Psalm 63:1-2
   2. God's power revealed in the Savior
     a) Explained
     b) Expressed
       (1) Matthew 9:8
       (2) Matthew 10:1
       (3) Matthew 28:18
       (4) Mark 9:1
       (5) Luke 4:32, 36
       (6) Romans 1:4
       (7) 1 Corinthians 1:24

Lesson
I. The Particulars
A. The Departure of the Disciples
   1. The following described
   2. The followers defined
     a) By context
       (1) Matthew 5:1
       (2) Matthew 8:21
       (3) John 15:6
       (4) Matthew 13:18-23
       (5) Matthew 10:22

Introduction

A. The Fall into Sin

When God created man, He ordained him to be king of the earth. But when man fell into sin, he was dethroned, losing his right to rule along with the majesty and glory of an innocent earth. God immediately cursed the earth, and as a result, its control fell into the hands of the usurper, Satan, who is called "the prince of this world" (John 12:31) and "the god of this age" (2 Cor. 4:4). How did that affect man? It brought sickness, pain, death, difficulty in human relationships, war, sorrow, injustice, falsehood, famine, natural disaster, and demonic activities. Those consequences have plagued the earth ever since.

B. The Future of Salvation

The Bible also unfolds for us a glorious redemptive plan. God is not only redeeming man, He is also restoring man's environment as well by reversing the curse. In order to accomplish that, God will come to earth twice—the first time to redeem man and the second time to redeem the earth and the universe. At His first coming, the Lord Jesus Christ went to the cross and rose from the grave for the redemption of man. The second time, He will come in blazing glory and establish a thousand-year (millennial) kingdom, which will be followed by a new heaven and a new earth. God will ultimately bring about a universe with no sorrow, tears, pain, sickness, death, disease, difficulties, disasters, or demons. In His coming kingdom, everything will be glorious forever, because the curse will have been reversed. Everything we know of as a curse will be changed in the future. Things that blight man's existence and steal his joy, things that take away from the dominion that God intended him to have, will be done away. The Bible even says that we will reign forever with Christ.

C. The Futility of Society

As we look toward the redemption of the earth in the coming glorious kingdom of God, it becomes obvious to us that man can't effect that change. We are limited in the things we can change in our environment. We can try to deal with some of the problems, but we can't eliminate them—we don't have the power. We may be able to shoot off rockets into space and build all kinds of machinery and equipment, yet still we pollute our environment. A medical doctor once told me that for everything in medicine that we solve, we create six other problems that must be solved. So the faster we seem to be progressing, the more we actually get behind. Man cannot bring about a renewed earth; he cannot eliminate the curse—he doesn't have the power. As clever as we are in dealing with energy sources, we still cannot harness and apply that power to changing our environment.

D. The Force of the Supernatural

If the earth is going to be changed and there's going to be a new heaven and a new earth, then that will have to be done by somebody far superior to any man. In fact, that power is not only beyond man; it is inconceivable to him. We can't imagine the kind of power it will take to reverse the curse, any more than we can imagine the kind of power that God had to create all things in the beginning and uphold His creation.

1. God's power recited in Scripture

   a) Psalm 62:11—"Power belongeth unto God."

   b) Job 26:14—"But the thunder of his power, who can understand?"

   c) Psalm 79:11—"The greatness of thy power."

   d) Nahum 1:3—"The Lord is . . . great in power."

   e) Isaiah 26:4—"In the Lord God is everlasting strength."

   f) Psalm 65:6—"Who by his strength setteth fast the mountains, being girded with power."

g) Psalm 63:1-2—"O God, thou art my God, early will I seek thee; my soul thirsteth for thee, my flesh longeth for thee . . . to see thy power."

2. God's power revealed in the Savior

   a) Explained

   What kind of power does God have? To a certain degree, it is visible to us through what God has created (Rom. 1:20). The Lord has the power to recreate the earth and reverse the curse. And I believe Jesus came to show us that power. He came into the world to declare that He is God the Son and that He has the power to bring the kingdom of God to a cursed earth. He came to show that He is the promised King and Messiah who could give back sovereignty to man by restoring the earth and eliminating sin.

   Jesus had all the necessary credentials. Matthew 1 informs us that He had the right genealogy—He was of the line of Abraham and David. In Matthew 2, we see that He had the right birth—He was born of a virgin. Matthew 3 tells us He had the right baptism—He was affirmed by the Father and anointed by the Spirit. Then in chapter 4, we find that He had the right test—the temptation scene showed His power over Satan. In Matthew 5-7, we see that He gave the right message—He confirmed the Word of God with absolute authority. That brings us to Matthew 8, where He is shown to have the right power. That theme carries over into the next chapter, where we read, "Ye may know that the Son of man hath power" (v. 6). The primary purpose of the miracles was to show that Jesus had power.

   The miracles were foretastes of kingdom power. When Jesus healed the sick, He was giving a preview of a glorious kingdom where there would be no sickness. When He raised the dead, He was giving a preview of a glorious kingdom where there would be no dying. When He calmed the waves on the sea, He was previewing a glorious kingdom where natural elements would never be out of control. When He cast out demons, He was previewing a kingdom where there would be no demonic activity at all. When He spoke the truth, He was previewing a kingdom where there would be no lies but only truth. When He manifested His holiness, He was previewing a kingdom where there would be only righteousness. Everything He did declared to man, "I am the One who can reverse the curse and restore sovereignty to man in a glorified eternal kingdom."

   b) Expressed

   The New Testament makes clear that Christ has divine power.

   (1) Matthew 9:8—"But when the multitudes saw it, they marveled, and glorified God, who had given such power unto men."

(2) Matthew 10:1—"And when he had called unto him his twelve disciples, he gave them power against unclean spirits, to cast them out, and to heal all manner of sickness and all manner of disease." Those two kinds of miracles are the only ones that the apostles had power to perform. They were never able to do miracles that dealt with nature—only Jesus did those.

(3) Matthew 28:18—"All authority [power] is given unto me."

(4) Mark 9:1—"And he said unto them, Verily I say unto you, There be some of them that stand here, who shall not taste of death, till they have seen the kingdom of God come with power." What was Jesus talking about? He was telling His disciples that some of them would see Him transfigured into His kingly splendor. That occurred a few days later when he was joined by Moses and Elijah on the Mount of Transfiguration.

(5) Luke 4:32, 36—"And they were astonished at his doctrine; for his word was with power. . . . And they were all amazed, and spoke among themselves, saying, What a word is this! For with authority and power he commandeth the unclean spirits."

(6) Romans 1:4—Jesus was "declared to be the Son of God with power . . . by the resurrection from the dead."

(7) 1 Corinthians 1:24—"Christ the power of God."

Matthew is showing us that Jesus Christ has power over every facet of the curse—disease and death, Satan and demons, natural elements, and everything else; therefore qualifying Himself as the rightful heir to the earth, the King of kings and Lord of lords.

Of the nine miracles in Matthew 8-9, we have already seen the first three, which dealt with disease. The next three show Jesus' power over natural elements, the supernatural world, and sin. All of those marvelously picture His power. Matthew presents a format of three miracles and a response. The response of the people to the first set of miracles is recorded in verses 18 to 22. The first group was thrilled with Christ's power. But when Jesus told them about the difficulties they could expect if they chose to follow Him, they went away. Now we move into the second set of miracles, which will end with a different response. Let us set the scene.

Lesson

I. THE PARTICULARS (vv. 18, 23-24)

A. The Departure of the Disciples (vv. 18, 23)

"Now, when Jesus saw great multitudes about him, he gave commandment to depart unto the other side. . . . And when he was entered into a boat, his disciples followed him."

1. The following described

The pressure of the crowd had reached a point where Jesus could no longer effectively minister. So He made a decision to leave the western shore of the Sea of Galilee, a lake thirteen miles long and eight miles wide. Jesus was tired after a full day of healing and teaching. It was late evening by the time His little boat left the shore by Capernaum to sail to the other side, and it was accompanied by several other little boats, according to Mark. Such boats were common in an area that was dependent upon fishing.

2. The followers defined

By that time, Mark and Luke tell us Jesus had already selected the twelve disciples, and it is very likely that a portion of them were in the boat with Him. But the reference to the disciples following Him indicates that many others were following Him as well. *Disciples* is a broad word. The context determines how it is to be interpreted in the New Testament. By itself, the Greek word *mathētēs* only identifies one who is a pupil, learner, or follower. Some believe that it refers to a second-level Christian who has a higher category of spirituality. In other words, there are plain Christians, and then there are disciples, the supersaints. But you cannot make the word mean that.

a) By context

(1) Matthew 5:1—"And seeing the multitudes, he went up into a mountain: and when he was seated, his disciples came unto him." What disciples? Some people think that Jesus gave the Sermon on the Mount to the twelve. But that sermon is a message on salvation, and it assumes that those listening may not have believed. Hence, in that context, "disciples" simply means "learners." It identifies a multitude of people who were interested in what Jesus had to say. Their level of commitment was undetermined at that point.

(2) Matthew 8:21—One "disciple" said, in effect, "I'm not going to follow You until my father dies." The implication is that he didn't go with Jesus, but turned around and went home. Being a disciple only meant that one was a learner, not necessarily a committed believer.

(3) John 15:6—Christ said that any branch that did not bear fruit would be cut off and thrown in the fire. There were some disciples who were connected with Christ but had no fruit of righteousness—nothing to mark true salvation—and were therefore separated from Christ. They were followers, but they weren't believers.

(4) Matthew 13:18-23—There were four types of soils, or disciples, that were following Jesus. Only one soil enabled

the seed to mature and become productive. One was real; three were not.

(5) Matthew 10:22—Jesus said that true disciples endure to the end. On that basis, Judas showed that he wasn't a true disciple.

There were many who learned from Jesus, but just because they were called disciples doesn't mean that they were believers. The word in itself only indicates that people were attracted to Jesus' teaching and were listening to it.

b) By category

We could reduce all disciples into four categories.

(1) The curious

Curious disciples followed Jesus in fascination. They were intrigued by what He said. But Jesus said to them, "Unless you are willing to affirm My total lordship in your life you cannot be My disciple or enter My kingdom." Not willing to make a full commitment to Christ, "Many of his disciples went back, and walked no more with him" (John 6:66).

(2) The committed

In contrast, the twelve showed that they were more than just followers. When Jesus asked them, "Will ye also go away?" Peter replied, "Lord, to whom shall we go? Thou hast the words of eternal life. And we believe and are sure that thou art the Christ, the Son of the living God" (John 6:67-69). In other words, Peter said, "We're not the kind of disciples who are just curious; we're the kind who are committed. We know that You speak the truth."

(3) The convinced

These were the disciples who were intellectually convinced. Nicodemus is a classic illustration. Having listened to what Jesus said and having seen what He did, Nicodemus came to Him by night and said, "You must be from God." He was intellectually convinced, but he didn't believe in Christ in the fullest sense then because he didn't forsake all to follow Him.

(4) The clandestine

There were some disciples like Joseph of Arimathea who kept their belief a secret.

In its broad usage, the word *disciples* can include Peters, Judases, Nicodemuses, and Josephs, as well as many others who would flee the first time things got tough. The word doesn't signify anything specific.

So all categories of disciples were following Jesus, and He was about to put on a display for them that was absolutely beyond belief.

B. The Storm on the Sea (v. 24)

1. The crisis (v. 24*a*)

"And, behold, there arose a great tempest in the sea, insomuch that the boat was covered with the waves."

Traveling in relatively small, open boats without any protection, Jesus and many disciples crossed the Sea of Galilee. That sea is actually a lake several hundred feet below sea level. Its water empties into the Jordan River and is carried southward to the Dead Sea, which is over one thousand feet below sea level. When cool air from the West and from Mount Hermon in the North collides with warm air above the Sea of Galilee, strong winds are forcefully drawn down the ravines and valleys that border the lake. Such a condition can create incredible storms in a very short period of time. Once those winds hit the cliffs on the eastern shore, they begin to swirl and whip in the little sea basin, often coming without any warning at all. I will never forget my own experience of getting on a boat in Capernaum when the water was like glass. But by the time we reached the middle, there were whitecaps billowing everywhere, and water was breaking over the bow, drenching people in the stern.

In the dark of night, "there arose a great tempest" (Gk., *seismos,* "a great quaking or shaking"). The Greek word used in the accounts of Mark and Luke is different; it means, "a whirlwind or storm." The indication of the text in the exclamation "behold" is that the storm was an unusually severe one. In other words, those fishermen had seen lots of storms, but not one like that.

2. The calmness (v. 24*b*)

"But he was asleep."

Anybody who could sleep through that was obviously very tired. That speaks to me of Jesus' humanness. He was so tired, even a storm couldn't wake Him up. Of course, His sleeping was a part of the divine plan, as was the storm that was tossing the boat like a cork on the ocean. And while the Creator of the world was peacefully asleep, the boat was filling up with water (Mark 4:37). We see here the reality of Christ's humanity as well as the fearless confidence He had in His Father's care. Oh, that we could live like that! We get tossed around by circumstances, begin to mistrust God, and panic. The heart of Jesus was perfectly calm in His peaceful assurance of God's care.

The sailors did everything possible to keep the boats afloat. Realizing the futility of their efforts, they finally came to Jesus. Now when sailors ask a former carpenter what to do in a storm, you know they are in a lot of trouble.

II. THE PANIC (vv. 25-26*a*)

A. The Request (v. 25)

"And his disciples came to him, and awoke him, saying, Lord, save us; we perish."

1. Examined

Mark records a statement that is just as terse, "Master, carest thou not that we perish?" (4:38*b*). In desperation they cried, "We're drowning out here; wake up!" Amazed at such apparent indifference, the disciples were not so much convinced that Christ was God as they were merely hoping that He was. But that was where God wanted them. Sometimes the Lord has to make us desperate to get our attention, doesn't He? They had run out of human resources. Now they needed a divine solution. They hoped that the miracle worker who could heal sickness could also handle the sea. They had fear mixed with faith. If they would have had total faith, they would have been like Jesus—confident in the Father's care.

The scene couldn't be more dramatic. The disciples broke in on Jesus' sleep in the same way men come to Him in desperate situations. They are like the sea captain who didn't believe there was a God, but when he got washed overboard, began to cry out for Him. His rescuers later questioned him, "We thought you didn't believe in God." "Well, if there isn't a God," he replied, "there ought to be one for times like that!" Many of us cry to God in desperation when sickness, disease, death, loss of a job, or marital problems afflict us. Even salvation is an act of God in response to the desperation of a sinner. But often our first cry is like that of the disciples' as recorded in Mark: "Don't you care? We're drowning!" If you have ever said that, you have demonstrated a lack of faith in God. You don't fully understand His love. Many saints of old suffered from similar lapses of faith.

2. Exemplified

a) Psalm 10:1—"Why standest thou afar off, O Lord? Why hidest thou thyself in times of trouble?" Paraphrased it might read, "God, You're never around when I need you; don't You care?"

b) Psalm 44:22-23—"Yea, for thy sake are we killed all the day long; we are counted as sheep for the slaughter. Awake, why sleepest thou, O Lord?" "How can You be sleeping through this when we're dying for You?"

c) Isaiah 51:9, 10—"Awake, awake, put on strength, O arm of the Lord; awake, as in the ancient days. . . . Was it not thou who hast dried the sea, the waters of the great deep; who hath made the depths of the sea a way for the ransomed to pass over?" The prophet is saying, "Get up, God. Don't You see the terrible dilemma of Your people? How can You possibly sleep through that?"

Those responses to trials are not unlike ours.

B. The Reply (v. 26a)

"And he saith unto them, Why are ye fearful, O ye of little faith?"

1. Examined

You can imagine that some of the disciples might have said, "You've got to be kidding; what kind of question is that? It's the middle of the night, we're in a storm like we've never seen before, and the boat is full of water!" The Greek word for "fearful" means "cowardly." Revelation 21:8 indicates that cowardliness is sin, and the same root word is used in the list of sinners who will not enter the kingdom. In fact, Mark records Jesus as saying, "How is it that ye have no faith? (4:40). Someone with such a lack of faith is guilty of doubting God's love and power. If you believe in those two key attributes of God, you can weather any storm, because you know that God cares about you and that He can handle any situation.

The disciples were questioning Jesus' care and ability to help them. Evidently their response surprised Jesus, because they had seen Him perform all kinds of miracles (Matt. 4:23-24). He cast out demons with only a word and was healing all that were sick. If the disciples didn't know He cared about human suffering, then they were blind. And if they didn't think He had the power to help them, they were ignorant.

Isn't is amazing how we can see a demonstration of God's love and power but, in certain circumstances, forget about those things? We witness the wonderful deeds that the Lord has done over and over again, and yet, as soon as something tough happens in our lives, we begin to question His love and power.

The disciples finally learned that they didn't have enough faith, so in Luke 17:5 they say, "Increase our faith." Not long after their request, Jesus healed ten lepers. What a faith builder that would have been! Faith needs constant strengthening. When our faith is "little," we distrust God's ability and loving care, refusing to believe that He can and will provide for our needs. That causes us to worry and become fearful. But if we know that He cares about us and is able to help, what do we have to fear?

2. Exemplified

Even if the disciples were drowning, they shouldn't have been afraid, because that would have apparently been God's will, and Christ would have delivered them into His Father's kingdom. Furthermore, they shouldn't have been afraid because they surely knew psalms like

a) Psalm 89:8-9—"O Lord God of hosts, who is like Thee, O mighty Lord? Thy faithfulness also surrounds Thee. Thou dost rule the swelling of the sea; when its waves rise, Thou dost still them" (NASB).

b) Psalm 46:1-3—"God is our refuge and strength, a very present help in trouble. Therefore will not we fear, though the earth be removed, and though the mountains be carried into the midst of the sea; though the waters thereof roar and be troubled, though the mountains shake with the swelling thereof."

c) Psalm 107:23-30—"Those who go down to the sea in ships, who do business on great waters; they have seen the works of the Lord, and His wonders in the deep. For He spoke and raised up a stormy wind, which lifted up the waves of the sea. They rose up to the heavens, they went down to the depths; their soul melted away in their misery. They reeled and staggered like a drunken man, and were at their wits' end. Then they cried to the Lord in their trouble, and He brought them out of their distresses. He caused the storm to be still, so that the waves of the sea were hushed. Then they were glad because they were quiet; so He guided them to their desired haven" (NASB). That's an implicit prophecy of what Jesus did. God provided deliverance from the storm in Psalm 107; Jesus did that in Matthew 8. Therefore, the conclusion is unarguable: Jesus is God. If the disciples had understood that, they would have had nothing to fear.

III. THE POWER (v. 26*b*)

"Then he arose, and rebuked the winds and the sea; and there was a great calm."

William Cowper, the English poet and hymnist, penned these great lines in his hymn, "God Moves in a Mysterious Way":

> God moves in a mysterious way
> His wonders to perform;
> He plants His footsteps in the sea
> And rides upon the storm.
> Ye fearful saints fresh courage take;
> The clouds ye so much dread
> Are big with mercy and shall break
> In blessings on your head.

Mark 4:39 says that Jesus stood up and commanded the storm to be silent. Instantly there was a great calm. Normally, if the wind stopped, the sea would have continued to ripple until the waves had run their course. But when Jesus said, "Hush" (NASB), the sea became as glass, as both the wind and the waves stopped. Now that's power! It's impossible to measure the power of the wind in that kind of a storm, because we don't know how far the storm extended. But in a normal storm, there are millions of units of horsepower generated through wind, and even more if there is rain. Jesus was able to stop that storm with a mere word. Matthew's message to us is that the One who conquers disease also controls nature. He later shows us that Christ also controls the demons, forgives sin, and raises the dead.

Having seen God, how did the disciples react? Because the dictionary says that something portentous elicits wonder or amazement, the final point has been titled:

IV. THE PORTENT (v. 27)

"But the men marveled, saying, What manner of man is this, that even the winds and the sea obey him?"

A. Expressed

Mark's parallel account says that when the storm came, the disciples were "fearful" (4:40). And when Jesus stopped the storm "they feared exceedingly" (4:41). Do you know what's more fearful than being in a storm? Realizing you're standing in the presence of the living God. That must have been awesome! What an experience to know that God was in their boat—that was far more terrifying than any storm.

B. Exemplified

1. By Job

When Job saw God through the circumstances of his life, he said, "I have heard of thee by the hearing of the ear, but now mine eye seeth thee. Wherefore I abhor myself, and repent in dust and ashes" (42:5-6).

2. By Isaiah

When Isaiah saw God, he said, "I am a man of unclean lips" (6:5).

3. By Daniel

When Daniel saw God, he began to shake and quiver and fell into a heap in the dirt. His mouth was frozen in dumbness in the presence of God (10:7-9).

4. By Peter

When Peter realized the divine power of Jesus after he had a miraculous catch of fish, he said, "Depart from me; for I am a sinful man, O Lord" (Luke 5:8).

5. By Paul

When the apostle Paul saw God in the form of a resurrected, glorious Jesus Christ, he fell on his face in the dirt and was blinded (Acts 9:3-9).

You, too, would be overwhelmed with God's holiness if you were to stand in His presence. The disciples knew that God was with them, and that reality was terrifying. They were unmasked by the omniscient One who could read their every thought. The next boat trip they took involved a similar situation where Jesus stilled another storm. Matthew 14:33 contains their response, "Then they that were in the boat came and worshiped him, saying, Of a truth, thou art the Son of God." There was no doubt this time that Jesus was the Son of God.

Conclusion

Can Jesus reverse the curse? Does He have the power to change the earth and restore the kingdom? The answer is yes. A songwriter has written these appropriate words:

> We sing th' Almighty pow'r of God who bade the mountains rise,
> Who spread the flowing seas abroad and built the lofty skies.

> We sing the wisdom that ordained the sun to rule the day;
> The moon shines, too, at His command and all the stars obey.

> Lord, how Thy wonders are displayed where e'er we turn our eyes
> When e'er we view the ground we tread or gaze upon the skies.

> There is not a plant nor flower below but makes Thy glories known;
> And clouds arise and tempest blow by order from Thy throne.

> On Thee each moment we depend; if Thou withdraw we die.
> Oh, may we ne'r that God offend who is forever nigh.

The same Jesus Christ who stilled the sea, keeps the earth whirling in space and the entire universe in balance, will return one day and set up His eternal kingdom. Will you be a part of that kingdom by faith in Him?

Focusing on the Facts

1. When God created man, what did He ordain man to be? What did man lose when he fell into sin? Whose control did the earth fall into? As a result, what are some of the consequences that have plagued the earth (see p. 51)?

2. What is the ultimate design of God for the universe (see p. 52)?

3. Taking into account man's inability to renew the earth, what is the only way that the curse can be reversed (see p. 52)?

4. According to Romans 1:20, how is God's power visible to us? By demonstrating His divine power, whom did Jesus show that He was, and what did He show that He was able to do (see p. 53)?

5. What were the miracles foretastes of (see p. 53)?

6. What were the people who followed Jesus in the boats called (see p. 55)?

7. Why can't the word *disciple* be used to mean a supersaint (see p. 55)?

8. Give examples for the four categories of disciples: curious, committed, convinced, and clandestine (see p. 56).

9. What can the land and weather conditions around the Sea of Galilee do in a very short period of time (see p. 57)?

10. What two things do we learn about Jesus from the incident of Him sleeping in the boat (see p. 57)?

11. What did Jesus reprove the disciples for? In effect, what two things were the disciples questioning about Jesus (see p. 59)?

12. According to the Old Testament, why shouldn't the disciples have been afraid (see pp. 59-60)?

13. What is all that Jesus had to do to calm the storm (see p. 60)?

14. From the disciples' perspective, what was evidently more fearful than being in a treacherous storm (see p. 61)?

15. Describe the general reactions of those who were found to be in the presence of God (see p. 61).

16. How did the disciples respond the next time Jesus stilled a storm (see p. 61)?

Pondering the Principles

1. Of the four kinds of disciples mentioned on page 56, in what category would you classify yourself? Why? There is a progression in the stages of discipleship. Which do you think occurs first? According to the parable of the sower, why do you think one cannot remain an intellectually convinced or a clandestine disciple for very long? What will a committed disciple evidence in his life (Matt. 5:3-12; 13:23; John 8:31)? If you are not yet a committed disciple, what is preventing you from being one? Find out if you don't know, and make the necessary changes. If you are one, help someone you know who is in one of the other three categories to become more spiritually mature.

2. Are you currently faced with a trial? What do you think God may be teaching you through it? Do you think He may just be trying to get your attention so that you can depend more upon Him? After meditating on 1 Corinthians 10:13, commit yourself to trusting Him in the situation at hand, realizing that the test you are experiencing has been made just for you.

3. Think of the time you last faced a crisis and didn't fully believe that Jesus cared about you or was able to help you. Meditate upon expressions of God's love and power in Psalm 103:2-6; John 17:10; 1 John 4:8-19; Jeremiah 32:17; Ephesians 1:18-21; and 3:20. Also, listen to or read the testimonies of how God has worked in the lives of others.

5
Jesus' Power over the Supernatural

Outline

Introduction
A. The Plan of God
B. The Proof of Christ
C. The Power over Satan
D. The Perspective of Men

Lesson
I. The Possession by Demons
  A. The Reception by Demons
    1. The place
    2. The possession
      a) Debated
      b) Delineated
      c) Defined
        (1) Adapting to society
        (2) Eclipsing personality
    3. The particulars
      a) Their residence
      b) Their irrationality
      c) Their rage
  B. The Recognition by the Demons
    1. Of Jesus' deity
    2. Of Jesus' authority
      a) James 2:19
      b) Luke 4:41
  C. The Requisition of the Demons
II. The Power of Christ
  A. The Method Exercised
  B. The Message Emphasized
III. The Perspective of the People
  A. The Reaction
  B. The Report
  C. The Request
    1. Explained
    2. Exemplified
      a) Isaiah 6:5

b) Luke 5:8

c) Mark 4:40-41

Conclusion

Introduction

This is a marvelous account familiar to many, and yet it is filled with meaning. Let us begin by reading verse 28 to the end of the chapter.

> "And when he was come to the other side into the country of the Gadarenes, there met him two possessed with demons, coming out of the tombs, exceedingly fierce, so that no man might pass by that way. And, behold, they cried out, saying, What have we to do with thee, Jesus, thou Son of God? Art thou come here to torment us before the time? And there was a good way off from them an herd of many swine feeding. So the demons besought him, saying, If thou cast us out, permit us to go away into the herd of swine. And he said unto them, Go. And when they were come out, they went into the herd of swine; and, behold, the whole herd of swine ran violently down a steep place into the sea, and perished in the waters. And they that kept them fled, and went their ways into the city, and told everything, and what was befallen to those possessed with the demons. And, behold, the whole city came out to meet Jesus; and when they saw him, they besought him that he would depart from their borders."

A. The Plan of God

God determines to redeem men, the earth, and the entire universe from the curse of sin. In order to do that, He came into the world in the form of the Messiah and saved man from sin and death. When Jesus Christ came to earth the first time, He accomplished the redemption of mankind. The second time He comes, He will redeem the earth and the universe around it. So Matthew is concerned that we understand that Jesus Christ is King of the earth, Messiah, the rightful ruler of the world, and the Son of God, the second member of the Trinity. In other words, we must see that the Lord Jesus Christ is God.

B. The Proof of Christ

One of the major ways of proving beyond a doubt that Christ is the Messiah is to show that He has power over the unseen forces of the supernatural world. If the Lord Jesus Christ will, in fact, redeem the earth and take possession of fallen humanity, He must show that He can overpower that which now holds all of creation in its control—Satan and his demons. Therefore, we find examples throughout the gospel record of Jesus' ability to cast out demons. He did that instantaneously and authoritatively, uttering only a word. That gives us clear proof that He can handle the kingdom of darkness.

C. The Power over Satan

We have already seen that Jesus Christ can resist Satan, for in Matthew chapter 4 Satan tempts Him, and the Lord is victorious—He confronts Satan and doesn't give in. But His power goes beyond that. The primary issue is not that Christ never gave in to Satan and his hosts; it is that He causes them to give in to Him.

Matthew has shown us the perfection of Christ in His temptation—He never gave in. Now we see the power of Christ—He makes the demons give in to Him. So Jesus manifests a resistant power as well as an overcoming power, demonstrating two dimensions of His ability to deal with the kingdom of darkness. First John 3:8 emphasizes the latter dimension, "For this purpose the Son of God was manifested, that he might destroy the works of the devil." Ultimately, when Jesus establishes His kingdom, He will incarcerate Satan and all his demon hosts for a thousand years. At the end, He will gather them up to be eternally tormented (Rev. 20:2, 10). By casting out demons throughout His ministry, Jesus was giving samples of His great power to destroy the works of the devil. In fact, on one occasion, He said, "But if I, with the finger of God, cast out demons, no doubt the kingdom of God is come upon you" (Luke 11:20). Why? Because one of the marks of the kingdom would be the overthrow of Satan, and Jesus was saying that if they saw Him doing it, they would know that the kingdom had come. So Christ came into the world to destroy the works of the devil. Matthew records that tremendous work in the eighth chapter of his gospel.

D. The Perspective of Men

The disciples themselves were aware that overthrowing Satan was not easy. In fact in Matthew 17:19, even though the Lord has given them power to cast out demons (Matt. 10:1), they have to admit that they can't get some demons to respond to them. So when Jesus comes along and casts out demons, the Bible says that people marveled. For example, Mark 1:27 says, "And they were all amazed, insomuch that they questioned among themselves, saying, What thing is this? What new doctrine is this? For with authority commandeth he even the unclean spirits, and they do obey him." It wasn't just that He cast them out—others may have had success with that at some point if they were godly people—it was the ease and the powerful authority with which He did it that shocked people. In fact, it was so unnatural, some concluded that Jesus was actually in collusion with demons, and the whole thing was a ruse. In Luke 11:15, the Pharisees accused Jesus, saying, "He casts out demons by the power of the prince of demons. That is a phony deal, folks; don't be kidded—that man is of the devil himself. Only if He were in collusion with the demons could He get such cooperation." They were forced to conclude that what He did was far beyond anything they had ever seen in their own experience.

Matthew shows us samples of Christ's power, desiring us to see that He is the One who can reverse the curse and set up the kingdom. He was able to heal sickness, control the forces of nature, deal with sin, overrule death, and conquer demons. Matthew records nine miracles in chapters 8 and 9 to show the

66

many facets of Christ's great power. I have outlined Matthew 8:28-34 with three key words: possession, power and perspective—the possession by demons, the power of Christ, and the perspective of the people.

Lesson

I. THE POSSESSION BY DEMONS (vv. 28-31)

After leaving Capernaum, Jesus and some of His disciples crossed the Sea of Galilee in a little boat. They encountered a storm, but the Lord calmed it. Then they continued on to the opposite shore, where they were immediately confronted by an incredible situation.

A. The Reception by Demons (v. 28)

"And when he was come to the other side into the country of the Gadarenes, there met him two possessed with demons, coming out of the tombs, exceedingly fierce, so that no man might pass by that way."

1. The place

The identity of the country of the Gadarenes on the other side of the Sea of Galilee has caused some confusion because Mark's account says "Gerasenes" (Mark 5:1) and some Greek manuscripts of Luke say "Gergesenes" (Luke 8:26). I believe the best explanation for the discrepancy is this: On the northeastern shore of the Sea of Galilee was a little village named *Gergesa* (or *Khersa,* as it is known today) about six miles from Capernaum. Its topography fits the story here, having cliffs that plunge down near the seas, where a herd of pigs could fall to their death. *Gadara,* a city much further south and inland, does not fit the setting. However, if we assume that Mark and Luke probably refer to Gergesa, the village, we can conclude that Matthew notes the whole area. The name *Gadara* could have not only referred to the city by that name, but also to the surrounding area that might have encompassed the village of Gergesa.

2. The possession

a) Debated

As the little boats arrived by divine appointment on the shore, "there met him two possessed with demons." Mark and Luke only introduce us to one of the two demoniacs. However, neither of them say here was only one. It is obvious there was two—one being the main figure with whom the dialogue of Mark 5 is carried on.

What does it mean to be possessed with demons or "demonized" (Gk., *daimonizomenos*)? Some people say that there's a difference between being obsessed, oppressed, and possessed. But the Bible doesn't make those distinctions. To be demonized simply means to be under the control of demons.

b) Delineated

Demons can tempt people to sin by getting into their minds and luring the thoughts. They can bring about disease, as in the case of Paul, who called the disorder that he had "a thorn in the flesh, the messenger of Satan to buffet me" (2 Cor. 12:7*b*). The Bible tells us that "doctrines of demons" (1 Tim. 4:1) pervert the truth and lead people into idolatry and error. Scripture delineates three areas of affliction with many New Testament illustrations.

(1) Physical affliction—disabling the body

    (*a*) Dumbness (Matt. 9:32-33)

    (*b*) Blindness (Matt. 12:22)

    (*c*) Deformity (Luke 13:11-17)

    (*d*) Epilepsy (Matt. 17:15-18)

(2) Mental affliction—deranging the mind

    (*a*) Insanity (Luke 8:27-29)

    (*b*) Suicidal mania (Mark 9:22)

    (*c*) Masochism (Mark 5:5)

    (*d*) Murder (Rev. 9:14-20; 18:2, 24)

(3) Spiritual affliction—driving to sinful practice

    (*a*) Corruption of the truth through false religion

    (*b*) Occult practices

    (*c*) Immorality

c) Defined

Although a definition of demon possession might be helpful, it can also be limiting. Remember that demonic activity is a supernatural reality, and we are not able to go any further than the Bible takes us in comprehending it. Demon possession is a condition in which one or more demons inhabit the body of a human being with the purpose of controlling it. There may be different degrees or manifestations of possession, however. The word *daimonizomenos* is used twelve times in the New Testament. So it is clear that both the Lord and the New Testament writers acknowledge its reality. In fact, in the early church, the gift of miracles or powers (Gk., *dunameōn;* 1 Cor. 12:10) included the ability to cast out demons.

(1) Adapting to society

In all of the incidents of demonizing in the New Testament, none of them are recorded as having occurred in the city of Jerusalem. I don't know if that's an important factor, but it seems to show that all of the incidents occurred in rural settings. Satan adapts himself to the level of sophistication in a society. Modern missionaries, for example, have stories about cases of demon possession, which are rather common in the rural setting that some of them work in, but are uncommon for us. Only once in my life have I been involved in a case of demon possession, where I actually talked with seven different demons speaking through a woman. But that is not a common occurrence. Demon possession seems to be most common in less sophisticated settings because in the presence of pagan religion, there is the fear of evil gods through which demons can exert their influence. However, when people in our society act demon possessed, we lock them up in an institution for the insane and try to ignore them. Therefore, demons don't have the same impact in our society, and that demands a much more subtle approach from satanic forces. But in the rural setting on the shore of the Sea of Galilee, demon-possessed maniacs were wreaking havoc.

(2) Eclipsing personality

The personality of a demon eclipses the personality of a demon-possessed person. In Mark's account, when Jesus asked a demoniac his name, the demon answered, "My name is Legion; for we are many" (5:9). The demoniac was unable to speak for himself. I witnessed the same thing when I was talking to the woman possessed by demons. When I asked a question, I got at least seven different voices, each with different names—she couldn't even speak in her own voice. Demon possession involves the automatic projection of an intense new personality. Now it may come and go, or it may be constant. I'm sure there are many people in our society who are diagnosed as mentally ill but are really possessed. And may I say that the solution for them is the same as it was for the demoniacs we meet in Matthew 8—the only One who has power over demons is the Lord Jesus Christ.

3. The particulars

   a) Their residence

   Verse 28 tells us that the demoniacs were living in tombs. To a Jewish person, one of the worst defilements of all was to touch a dead body. How far those poor souls must have been driven for them to be living in the tombs! The cliffs are high in that area of the eastern Galilean shore, and chambers had been hewn out of the rocks for use as tombs.

   b) Their irrationality

   We learn more about the demoniacs in parallel accounts. Luke 8:27 says that they "wore no clothes." There are people who have said things like, "There's nothing wrong with wearing no clothes; I belong to the Sunshine Nudist Colony." In the Bible, the only people who went around naked were raving maniacs, who had no sense of social balance or modesty.

c) Their rage

Matthew also says the demoniacs were "exceedingly fierce." That means they were violent. Mark 5 says that people had tried to bind them with chains, but those demoniacs broke them with their tremendous strength. Such strength was demonstrated to me when the demon-possessed woman I spoke with flipped over a steel desk with only two fingers. Mark also says they were "crying [Gk., *krazō,* "an inarticulate shriek"], and cutting [themselves] with stones" (v. 5). Can you visualize the scene? They were stark naked, hacking themselves with stones, shrieking, and racing down the hillside with incredible strength. No wonder that the end of Matthew 8:28 says, "so that no man might pass by that way." No one dared to go down that road, for as soon as they did, the demoniacs would come out of the tombs, screaming down the hillside.

B. The Recognition by the Demons (v. 29)

1. Of Jesus' deity (v. 29*a*)

"And, behold, they cried out, saying, What have we to do with thee, Jesus, thou Son of God?"

In other words, the demons who controlled those two men asked, "Why are you bothering us? Why are You here?" In fact, Mark 5:6 tells us that when they saw Jesus, they "ran and worshiped him." The Greek word is *proskuneō,* which describes a person who reverences a superior such as a king or supernatural being on his knees. It can contain the idea of profound awe, respect, and worship. It is incredible that the demons should bow before Jesus, but they did. Why did they do that? Because they knew exactly who He was. As fallen angels who participated in Satan's rebellion against God, demons are well acquainted with Him and with Jesus, His Son, the second Person of the Trinity. Nobody needs to help them with their Christology. Therefore, those particular demons knew that Jesus was their antagonist as well as their Judge.

Think of it—beings who were damned for all eternity and knew it, could not resist worshiping Him, because they knew of His ultimate power. I do not doubt that all demons know the truth of Philippians 2:10, which says "that at the name of Jesus every knee should bow, of things in heaven, and things in earth, and things under the earth."

2. Of Jesus' Authority (v. 29*b*)

"Art thou come here to torment us before the time?"

The demons realized that Jesus was there too soon to be judging them. They knew that Jesus was Christ, the Son of the living God (some cults don't even know what demons know); they knew what the eschatological plan was, and they knew that they were to be damned forever. Therefore, they bowed the knee to Christ, their Judge. Evidently, demons somehow have already been made aware of the divine plan and can even anticipate what is going to happen at some points. They were way ahead of the Lord's disciples in their understanding of both of Messiah's comings.

When the demons addressed Him as "Jesus, thou Son of God," they made an important statement. The title "Son of God" is a synonym for Messiah. In Matthew 16:16, Peter answered Christ, saying, "Thou art the Christ [Messiah, the Hebrew equivalent of the Greek], the Son of the living God." God the Father was revealing through Peter that the Messiah is the Son of the living God. It's clear that demons acknowledge God's authority and power.

a) James 2:19—"Thou believest that there is one God; thou doest well. The demons also believe, and tremble." Rightly so, because they know the end result of their rebellion.

b) Luke 4:41—"And demons also came out of many, crying out, and saying, Thou art Christ [Messiah], the Son of God. . . . for they knew that he was Christ."

C. The Requisition of the Demons (vv. 30-31)

"And there was a good way off from them an herd of many swine feeding. So the demons besought him, saying, If thou cast us out, permit us to go away into the herd of swine."

The demons knew it was inevitable that they would be cast out, because they also knew of Christ's compassion for those whom they held captive. Consequently, they made a strange request. They wanted to inhabit a herd of two thousand pigs (Mark 5:13). One wonders why they would request such a thing. We don't really know, but maybe the demons, desiring a home, thought that their request to possess the pigs would be an acceptable concession to Jesus, who didn't want the demons harming people. Most probably, the demons feared being sent to the bottomless pit (Luke 8:31). Possibly they wanted to destroy the pigs so people would kill Jesus for having brought about the slaughter of the herd. We can only speculate. But whatever the reason, the demons had their plan. And Jesus' response is most interesting.

II. THE POWER OF CHRIST (v. 32)

Matthew now takes our focus off the demons and onto Christ, "And he said unto them, Go. And when they were come out, they went into the herd of swine; and, behold, the whole herd of swine ran violently down a steep place into the sea, and perished in the waters."

A. The Method Exercised

When men try to cast out demons, they work hard to get the demons to cooperate, but when Christ comes along, all the demons want to know is where they're allowed to go. He simply said, "Go," and the entire herd of two thousand pigs rushed off the cliff into the sea below and drowned. When He appeared, they wanted to leave, and so He commanded them to do so with only one word. That instantaneous miracle shocked everybody. It wasn't necessarily what He did; it was primarily *how* He did it.

Realizing that demons are powerful beings and that men cannot effectively deal with them on the supernatural level, one can see how ludicrous it is for people to think they can cast out demons by their cleverness. People are no match for the power of demons. Second Peter 2:11 says that "angels . . . are greater in power and might" than men. Psalm 103:20 says that "angels . . . excel in strength." One holy angel in 2 Kings 19:35 slew 185,000 Assyrians at one time. Evidently, demons are as powerful as holy angels, for Daniel 10:13 indicates that a holy angel, who was dispatched with a message from God for Daniel, was withstood by a demon for three weeks until Michael came to assist him. Demons are incredibly powerful. Therefore, the only way that man can handle them is by putting on the armor of God and being strong "in the power of his might" (Eph. 6:10-11). Only the power of the Lord Jesus Christ could cast demons into the bottomless pit (Rev. 20:3), and He displayed His power by casting them into swine.

B. The Message Emphasized

Jesus granted the demons their request, however, not for their sake, but for His. He allowed them to enter the herd of pigs. In trying to determine why Jesus granted that request, some people say that Jesus was teaching a lesson to people who were raising pigs when they shouldn't have. However, I don't think that is the lesson here. The primary point is that Christ can cast out demons, and He gave a dramatic demonstration of His ability. The reality of His miracle was clear to those observing when a normally peaceful herd of pigs demonically raced toward a cliff, dove in the water, and drowned. At the same time, the individuals that had previously been demonized were "sitting, and clothed, and in [their] right minds" (Mark 5:15). The bystanders saw a deliverance they would never forget. Furthermore, Jesus' exorcism portrayed the destructive nature of demons and also gave them a preview of their coming destruction. So if you're concerned about the pigs, you've missed the point. We must be willing to allow the sacrifice of two thousand pigs for Jesus to manifest His incredible power. I believe that He wanted living proof that the demons came out of the men—and what unforgettable proof He gave!

III. THE PERSPECTIVE OF THE PEOPLE (vv. 33-34)

A. The Reaction (v. 33*a*)

"And they that kept them fled, and went their ways into the city."

That verse refers to the swineherds, the people who cared for the pigs out on the hills. When they saw that their pigs had committed mass suicide by racing like maniacs into the water, they took off for the city as fast as they could go.

B. The Report (v. 33b)

"And told everything, and what was befalled to those possessed with the demons."

Notice that the swineherds got the message. They didn't emphasize what had happened to the pigs; the issue was the men who were delivered from the demons. The pigs' fate was only the proof.

C. The Request (v. 34)

"And, behold, the whole city came out to meet Jesus; and when they saw him, they besought him that He would depart from their borders."

1. Explained

   The city didn't come out to Jesus to participate in a revival, as their request reveals. Some think that they said what they did because they were more concerned about their pigs than Jesus, being consummate materialists unconcerned about the souls of the demonized men. But that reasoning is weak because the passage doesn't say a word about the owners of the pigs. The response is that of the whole city. Mark 5:15 says, "They were afraid." They were not angry; they were scared to death. Luke 8:37 similarly says, "They were taken with great fear."

   The principle we see here is that when unholy men face a holy God, they experience terror.

2. Exemplified

   a) Isaiah 6:5—"Woe is me! For I am undone . . . for mine eyes have seen the King, the Lord of hosts." Isaiah, the best man in the land, pronounced a curse on himself when he saw God, because his unholiness was exposed.

   b) Luke 5:8—"When Peter saw Jesus Christ in the majesty of His power, he said, "Depart from me; for I am a sinful man, O Lord."

   c) Mark 4:40-41—When a severe storm came, the disciples were "fearful," and when Jesus stilled the storm, they "feared exceedingly." They were more afraid of the calm than they were of the storm, because they knew that God was in their boat.

   The supernatural power of Jesus caused the townspeople to panic, because they observed the One who not only controlled the demons, but also took the souls of two men and gave them back to them. Supernatural things make men uncomfortable. The people from the city were absolutely panicked by the presence of Jesus in their midst. Instead of falling at His feet in worship, they said, "Go away; we don't want You!"

People think that if everybody could see miracles, they would believe. Unfortunately, many of the people who saw the miracles of Christ didn't believe—they nailed Him to a cross instead. Some people, when exposed to the awesomeness of a holy God, want nothing to do with Him because they love their darkness. They are like bugs under a rock that run for cover as soon as they are exposed to light.

Conclusion

The story isn't over—it ends in Mark 5:18-20, where we see how gracious God was to the people of Decapolis; "And when he was come into the boat, he that had been possessed with the demon implored him that he might be with him. Howbeit, Jesus permitted him not, but saith unto him, Go home to thy friends, and tell them what great things the Lord hath done for thee, and hath had compassion on thee. And he departed, and began to publish in Decapolis what great things Jesus had done for him; and all men did marvel." The fearful people who wanted Jesus out of their country never did break His compassion or mercy for them, for He left them at least one missionary as living proof of His mighty power. How wonderful that the grace of Christ is extended even to those who don't want it!

Focusing on the Facts

1. What does Matthew want us to understand about Jesus Christ as he writes his gospel (see p. 65)?

2. If the Lord Jesus Christ is to redeem the earth and take possession of fallen humanity, what must He overpower (see p. 65)?

3. What are the two kinds of power that Jesus manifests with regard to Satan (see p. 66)?

4. What is one of the purposes that Christ came to earth, according to 1 John 3:8 (see p. 66)?

5. What is the ultimate fate of Satan and his demons (Rev. 20:2, 10; see p. 66)?

6. What was the general reaction of the people who saw Jesus cast out demons? Why (Mark 1:27; see p. 66)?

7. How can the discrepancy between the different names of the place where the demoniacs dwelt be resolved (see p. 67)?

8. Did Jesus meet one or two demoniacs? Explain (see p. 67).

9. In what three areas do demons afflict people (see p. 68)?

10. Why might cases of demon possession be relatively uncommon except in rural areas (see pp. 68-69)?

11. Why would no man pass by the area where the demoniacs lived (Matt. 8:28b; see p. 70)?

12. Why did the demoniacs bow before Jesus (see p. 70)?

13. Who did the Father reveal Christ to be through the apostle Peter (Matt. 16:16; see p. 71)?

14. What are two possible reasons the demons wanted to be sent into the swine (see p. 71)?

15. How did Jesus cast the demons out (see pp. 71-72)?

16. What is the primary point of the dramatic demonstration that Jesus gave (see p. 72)?

17. What did the report of the swineherds emphasize (see p. 73)?

18. Why did the people from the city ask Jesus to leave, according to Mark 5:15 (see p. 73)?

19. Why are miracles not a guarantee that people will believe (see p. 74)?

20. According to Mark 5:18-20, how did God demonstrate His grace to the cities of Decapolis (see p. 74)?

Pondering the Principles

1. Has your faith been shaken by someone who seemed to know more about the Bible than you did and discredited the biblical account? In your Bible reading, you have probably come across several apparent contradictions between parallel accounts of an incident. When you encounter them, put a question mark by them so that you can make a more detailed study that can provide some reasonable solutions. A church library or your local Christian bookstore may have several commentaries on the passage in question or books that specifically deal with Bible difficulties. Many times there are very simple explanations for apparent difficulties that historical, cultural, or geographical insights can help provide.

2. Demons are powerful, but we need not fear them as Christians, for we are indwelt by the Spirit of the One was has permanently sealed their defeat. Meditate on the following verses to learn how to effectively face the arch-enemy of God and his host: Matthew 4:1-11; Ephesians 6:10-18; James 4:4-7; 1 Peter 5:6-9; and 1 John 5:18.

6
Jesus' Power over Sin

Outline

Introduction
A. Surveying the Strategy of Matthew
   1. Presenting the identity of Jesus
   2. Presenting the ability of Jesus
      a) Over the physical realm
      b) Over the supernatural realm
      c) Over the spiritual realm
B. Setting the Scene of the Miracle
   1. The city
   2. The crowds
   3. The house

Lesson
I. Faith
   A. The People
   B. The Purpose
   C. The Problems
   D. The Persistence
   E. The Promise
II. Forgiveness
   A. Explained
   B. Exemplified
   C. Evaluated
      1. The sinfulness of man
      2. The forgiveness of God
III. Fury
   A. The Analysis of the Situation
   B. The Accuracy of the Statement
   C. The Accusations Against the Savior
      1. Blasphemous
      2. Immoral
      3. Impious
      4. Satanic
IV. Forensic
   A. Divine Perception
      1. 1 Samuel 16:7

Introduction

The Lord said, "Thy sins be forgiven thee" to a paralytic in Matthew 9:2. That phrase forms the theme of this particular passage, which is Jesus' power over sin. That power, seen in Jesus' authority to forgive, is the most distinctive message that Christianity has to proclaim. The reality that sin can be forgiven is the heart of the Christian message. Although the Christian faith has many virtues and myriad applications, the most essential message God ever gave is that sinful man can know the fullness of forgiveness. That is what we learn from the healing of the paralytic in Matthew 9.

A. Surveying the Strategy of Matthew

   1. Presenting the identity of Jesus

Matthew has been focusing on various miracles of our Lord in chapters 8 and 9 that are intended to present the deity of Jesus Christ and His role as the Messiah of Israel. In other words, Matthew records a series of miracles not only to prove that Jesus is God, but to show Jesus fulfilling Messianic prophecies and expectations so that Israel would know that He was the Messiah and would introduce the kingdom of God to the world. For that reason, there is an Old Testament character to the kind of miracles that Matthew selects under the inspiration of the Holy Spirit.

   2. Presenting the ability of Jesus

Jesus' ability over the following is the thrust of the second triad of miracles in Matthew 8 and 9.

     a) Over the physical realm

The first miracle of that second set was when Jesus stilled the storm. It fulfilled the Old Testament prophecies that predicted the Messiah would set up a kingdom and overpower the curse in the physical world. For example, Isaiah 30:23-24 says there will be an abundance of rain and crops that will flourish in ways never known since before the Fall. Isaiah 35:1-7 talks about the desert blossoming like a rose. Similar evidences of physical restoration are seen in Isaiah 41:17-18; 51:3; 55:13;

Joel 3:18; and Ezekiel 36:29-38. Animals that have been natural enemies will no longer be so. Life will lengthen, for if a person dies at a hundred years of age, he will be considered to have died young.

b) Over the supernatural realm

The Old Testament also speaks of a time when Satan will bring his great hosts against the people of God and be defeated. We find in Zechariah 3:1-2; Daniel 7:24-27; Daniel 8:23-25; and Daniel 11:36-12:3 that Satan wants to oppress the people of God and ultimately will send the demon forces and Antichrist to fight against God's people. Therefore, the Messiah must be able to overpower the supernatural world of demons and Satan himself, which is precisely what Matthew seeks to prove in showing that Jesus could cast out demons.

c) Over the spiritual realm

The Old Testament also tells us that the kingdom will be marked by forgiveness in such passages as Ezekiel 36: Isaiah 33:24; 40:1-2; and 44:21-22. And here in Matthew 9:1-8 we find that the Lord Jesus Christ, God in human flesh, is able to forgive sin.

Thus, Christ will establish the kingdom of God in the earth and throughout eternity. So those are not random miracles; they purposefully point to His power and the fulfillment of Old Testament promises. In fact, the accuracy of their fulfillment is so specific that it makes the unbelief and rejection of the Pharisees all the more unbelievable and heinous.

B. Setting the Scene of the Miracle

The setting for the third miracle of the second section begins in verse 1. "And he entered into a boat, and passed over, and came into his own city." We don't know how much time lapses between the end of chapter 8 and the beginning of 9, for Matthew is not as concerned with chronology as he is with using specific miracles to present Jesus as the Messiah.

1. The city

Having healed the demon-possessed men on the eastern shore of the Sea of Galilee, Jesus returned in the boat and came into His own city. Now you might think that Nazareth, where He grew up, was His city. However, if you read Matthew 4:13-15, you discover that He moved to Capernaum at the beginning of His ministry, "And leaving Nazareth, he came and dwelt in Capernaum, which is upon the seacoast, in the borders of Zebulun and Naphtali, that it might be fulfilled which was spoken by Isaiah." In fact, Luke 4:29-31 indicates that He left Nazareth because they threw Him out—He was a prophet without honor in His own country. He reestablished His home several miles away in the little town of Capernaum on the north shore of the Lake of Galilee. It is even likely that He had taken up residence in the house of Peter from such indications as Matthew 8:14-15, where He healed Peter's mother-in-law.

2. The crowds

Before He crossed the Lake of Galilee, Jesus had been doing miracles in Capernaum and the surrounding area. He had been healing all kinds of diseases and had been casting out demons. Such demonstrations of power had caused the crowds to swell wherever He went. As He came back, another huge crowd had come to the place where He stayed.

3. The house

It is marvelous that Matthew, Mark, and Luke each wrote about the same story and picked out different issues that were pertinent to their own purposes. For that reason, parallel accounts from Mark 2 and Luke 5 help us to see the whole picture. Jesus had gone into a house (possibly Peter's) and was probably upstairs. It was common in those days to build a two-story house and to use the large upper room for social gatherings. That seemed to be the case with the house in which He broke bread with His disciples on the night He was arrested. Then, on top of the house was a flat roof, where people could spend time as well. Because of the climate in that part of the world, the rooftop was a pleasant place to be. Homes that had such a roof would also have had outside staircases going up to it. Evidently, the Lord was in a house that may have been like that, and the people had crowded their way in. Perhaps the crowd even extended out the doors and onto the porch.

In that setting, we see a marvelous demonstration of faith and healing that we will examine under the heading of six key words.

Lesson

I. FAITH (v. 2a)

"And, behold, they brought to him a man sick of the palsy, lying on a bed; and Jesus, seeing their faith, said unto the sick of the palsy, Son, be of good cheer."

A. The People

First of all, notice that there is no antecedent in Matthew for the people who brought the paralytic. However, in Mark and Luke we find that there were four men, possibly friends or relatives, who brought that man in. Evidently they cared about him. They had all heard that Jesus was in town and wanted the paralytic to come to Jesus. The paralytic may have even recruited the four to help him.

B. The Purpose

The man needed to have someone bring him to Jesus, because he was "sick of the palsy" (Gk., *paralutikos*). That was a type of paralysis, which is a loss of the motor functions of the body and sometimes includes a loss of sensory ability. It could have been the result of a neck or back injury, a birth defect, muscular dystrophy, polio, or various other diseases. He may have had a severe paralysis that rendered him a quadriplegic. He was unable to assist those who moved him, for it took four men to carry him on a pallet, which was a thick quilt or a thin mattress that could be rolled up and carried about. It was often supported by a thin wooden frame.

C. The Problems

In Biblical times it would have been extremely difficult to be paralyzed, because the ambulatory apparatus and the medical knowledge that we have today was not available. A paralytic would have to be cared for in all of the basic necessities of life. As a result, there was probably even more of a social stigma attached to such disabling illnesses than there is now.

Futhermore, the paralytic probably thought that he was sick because he was sinful, a common conclusion of the time. You may remember some disciples asking Jesus about this issue, "Master, who did sin, this man, or his parents, that he was born blind?" (John 9:2). Now the disciples were right in the sense that all sickness is linked to sin, because if there were no sin, there would be no sickness. But they were wrong in reflecting the feeling of the day that a person became sick directly from being sinful. In fact, such thinking had been around for a long time, going all the way back to the book of Job (possibly the first Bible book ever written). Job's friends had essentially told Job that sin was his problem. Therefore, the paralytic not only suffered from the disease itself and the stigma and incapacitation that accompanied it, but also from an overwhelming sense that he was sinful, and therefore directly responsible for his illness. Although it would not be uncommon for such people to seek to be alone and shun the crowds, that man wanted to come to Jesus. I believe without any doubt that the paralytic came to Jesus primarily because of his sin, not his sickness. That is why Jesus said to him, "Son, be of good cheer; thy sins be forgiven thee" (v. 2b). Evidently, the despair of his life was not that he was physically ill, but that he was sinful.

Sickness is not always directly related to sin. However, all sickness is a graphic demonstration of the destructive power that's at work in the world because of sin. Whether or not the man understood how his sickness was related to his sin, as in the case of James 5:14-15, he did know that there was sin in his life that needed to be dealt with.

D. The Persistence

What makes the faith that Jesus recognized in the men who brought the paralytic so great? Evidently, they must have believed that Jesus could heal him, because they brought him to Jesus. According to the accounts of Mark and Luke, they came to the house where Jesus was but couldn't get in with the paralytic because of the crowd. So they decided that there was only one way to get in. They climbed the outside staircase, went up on the rooftop, and began to make a hole in the roof by removing tiles. They must have made some fairly good calculations because when they were done, they dropped the paralytic on his pallet straight down at Jesus' feet. That is persistent, inventive faith!

Even the paralytic had faith if we assume that he had enlisted the four men to bring him to Jesus. We can't know that from what he said, however, because he made no request at all. He may have been paralyzed to the extent that he couldn't talk. He laid at the feet of Jesus, in full view of everybody, full of grief and fear. He knew that Jesus was a healer of bodies, and I'm convinced that he must have hoped that He was also a healer of hearts. The thing that probably burdened him most was his sin. He willingly exposed the ugliness of his social stigma and his sinfulness to the whole crowd for the sake of being at the feet of Jesus. That's the true humility of a seeking heart. For that reason, I believe that Jesus recognized the faith of all five of them. Theirs was not an ordinary faith; it was strong and persistent. Although there were times when Jesus healed people with no faith at all or very little, He was especially disposed to healing people with great faith. For example, in Matthew 9:18 we read, "While he spoke these things unto them, behold, there came a certain ruler, and worshiped him, saying, My daughter is even now dead; but come and lay thy hand upon her, and she will live." To believe in resurrection involves great faith. In the same chapter, "Blind men came to him; and Jesus saith unto them, Believe ye that I am able to do this? They said unto him, Yea, Lord. Then touched he their eyes, saying, According to your faith be it unto you" (vv. 28-29). So Jesus was especially disposed to those of that kind of faith, and that paralytic had it even though he lay in silent reverence.

E. The Promise

The Lord broke the silence and said to the one who was paralyzed, "Son, be of good cheer [or, "take courage" (NASB)]." Jesus addressed the man as "Son" (Gk., *teknon,* "child"), a term of tenderness. Here was a man overwrought with his sin by social condemnation from without and the guilt from within. Believing that Jesus possessed the power of God, he was willing to put himself in the presence of a Holy God and take his chances. In the midst of his fear, the Lord said to him, "Stop being afraid—take courage! There's nothing to fear." In a wonderful way, the Lord comforted and encouraged one who was fearfully conscious of his sickness and sin. That's the tenderness of Christ, who can love the sinner even though He is offended by his sin.

The statement "be of good cheer" uses the Greek verb *tharseō,* which refers to a subjective courage. A synonymous verb *(tolmaō)* refers to a courage that is objective. It would be like saying, "Grit your teeth, hang on, and master your fear." But the word Jesus used means "there's nothing to be afraid of." In other words, the Lord didn't say to him, "Look fella, grit your teeth and master your fear"; He said, "Child, what are you afraid of? There is nothing to fear."

Let me tell you something. There's plenty to fear if you come before God as a sinner without repentance. But there was nothing to fear when the paralytic came, because he had a broken and contrite heart. The Lord doesn't forgive the sins of people who don't. It is not the one who tries to hide his sin who has nothing to fear; it is the one who reveals it that has nothing to fear. To this man who was shaken with grief, overcome with fear, and burdened with guilt, the Lord responded in answer to his faith.

II. FORGIVENESS (v. 2b)

A. Explained

Jesus said, "Your sins are dismissed." Forgiveness is a divine miracle that ranks with any other miracle—it is instantaneously bestowed with a word. If the paralytic had never said a word, how did the Lord know that forgiveness was what he wanted? Simply because the Lord knows the heart of every man. He read the heart of the paralytic, and He read the hearts of the scribes. As a giver of all good, He gives before we can even articulate the request. And the case of the paralytic was no different. He read the man's heart and dismissed his sins.

The remission of sins is an integral part of salvation. When the Lord sends our sins away, He sends them as far as the east is from the west, buries them in the depths of the deepest sea, and remembers them no more (Ps. 103:12; Mic. 7:19; Jer. 31:34b). In 1 Timothy 1, Paul said, "[I was] a blasphemer, and a persecutor, and injurious; but I obtained mercy. . . . This is a faithful saying, and worthy of all acceptance, that Christ Jesus came into the world to save sinners, of whom I am chief" (vv. 13, 15). The Lord gave the greatest gift that dealt with the greatest need.

B. Exemplified

When I was finishing my senior year at college, playing football, I spoke at a Kiwanis Club that was honoring me with an award. Somebody came up afterwards and asked me to talk to a girl in a hospital who had been accidently shot in the neck and paralyzed. So I went to the hospital and talked with her. She told me that she would kill herself if she could, but of course she was unable. After I had presented the gospel to her, she agreed to ask Christ into her life as we prayed together. I'll never forget what she said to me after I went back to see her: "I can honestly say that I'm glad the accident happened, because if it hadn't, I never would have met Christ and had my sins forgiven." That's the deepest need and the truest grief in a human life. When Jesus said, "Your sins are removed," He met that man's need in the most profound way. Forgiveness of sins is the message of Christianity.

C. Evaluated

People say, "You shouldn't bring up sin; that's negative thinking." But it's essential to the message of Christianity. If we don't talk about sin and the need for forgiveness, we have prostituted our message.

1. The sinfulness of man

The Bible says that sin:

a) Transgresses the law (1 John 3:4)

b) Defiles God's image in man—it has stained the soul with the devil's image (John 6:70; 8:44)

c) Rebels against God (Lev. 26:27)

d) Displays gross ingratitude toward God (Josh. 2:10-12)

e) Is incurable—Jeremiah 13 says, "Can the Ethiopian change his skin, or the leopard his spots? Then may ye also do good, that are accustomed to do evil" (v. 23)

f) Affects all men—"For all have sinned, and come short of the glory of God" (Rom. 3:23)

g) Is deep in the heart of man—even regenerate man still fights against it (Rom. 7:19)

h) Dominates the entire person—it perverts the mind, will, affections, and body (Jer. 17:9)

i) Brings man under the dominion of the devil (Eph. 2:2)

j) Brings man under the power of God's wrath (Eph. 2:3)

k) Subjects man to misery

(1) Sin causes trouble (Job 5:7)

(2) Sin causes emptiness (Rom. 8:20)

(3) Sin causes peace to be forfeited (Isa. 57:21)

l) Dooms men to hell forever (2 Thess. 1:9)

2. The forgiveness of God

If sin so affects all men, then the best news you could ever give is that God forgives sin. The paralytic was living proof. When Jesus said, "Thy sins be forgiven thee," I believe the pain of Calvary thrust into His great heart, because He knew that the only way He could forgive that man's sin was to bear it. In like manner, He must have tasted the agony of the cross throughout His life whenever He forgave sin. He knew He would bear the punishment that He had removed from that helpless soul.

III. FURY (v. 3)

"And, behold, certain of the scribes [along with some Pharisees (Luke 5:17)] said within themselves, This man blasphemeth." Mark and Luke add that they reasoned, "Who can forgive sins but God only?" (Mark 2:7; Luke 5:21).

A. The Analysis of the Situation

Jesus forgave the crippled man, but the scribes and Pharisees concluded that Jesus was a blasphemer. They even failed to acknowledge their need for forgiveness. Such an attitude has been around for a long time. Today, when a message is preached on forgiveness, some will open their hearts to Christ, and others will leave uninterested, failing to recognize the problem of sin and therefore not willing to accept the solution of forgiveness. Furthermore, instead of accepting the fact that Jesus could forgive sin and relieve the pressure of their guilt, Christ's opponents realized that since only God could forgive sin, and Jesus was claiming to be God, He was therefore a blasphemer. To them, the ultimate blasphemy was to claim to be God by saying and doing things that only could be ascribed to Him.

B. The Accuracy of the Statement

The scribes and Pharisees were right about the fact that only God can forgive sin: Isaiah 43:25 says, "I, even I, am he who blotteth out thy transgressions." However, they were wrong about Christ, because He is God. In fact, the divine ability Jesus demonstrated by reading their thoughts was evidence of His omniscience. He knew what was in the heart of the sick man, and He knew what was in the minds of the scribes and Pharisees, because He is God.

C. The Accusations Against the Savior

1. Blasphemous

When the scribes and Pharisees accused Jesus of blasphemy, it was part of the ever-increasing antagonism that ultimately led them to crucify Him.

2. Immoral

Verse 11 says, "And when the Pharisees saw it, they said unto his disciples, Why eateth your Master with tax collectors and sinners?" In other words, "If He runs around with a bad crowd, then He must be a bad man."

3. Impious

Verse 14 says, "Then came to Him the disciples of John, saying, Why do we and the Pharisees fast often, but thy disciples fast not?" Here were some accusing Him of being irreligious. He didn't follow the accepted religious practices.

4. Satanic

The culminating accusation of the chapter comes in verse 34, "But the Pharisees said, he casteth out demons through the prince of the demons." What a contrast their fury was in light of the faith of the paralytic and the four who helped him! That's always the way it is. Christ comes with a message of love, grace, and forgiveness, and there are those who rejoice in it and yet others who become infuriated by it.

IV. FORENSIC (vv. 4-6)

Forensic means "an argument," which is exactly what Jesus presented here. He didn't always defend His actions, but this time He did, because there was an important truth to be expressed.

A. Divine Perception (v. 4)

"And Jesus, knowing their thoughts, said, Why think ye evil in your hearts?"

People often say that Jesus isn't God. If He isn't, then I don't know how He knew men's thoughts. John 2:25 says that He "needed not that any should testify of man; for he knew what was in man." Anybody who knows people's thoughts must be God, as the following passages show.

1. 1 Samuel 16:7—"The Lord looketh on the heart."

2. 1 Kings 8:39—"For thou, even thou only, knowest the hearts of all the children of men."

3. 1 Chronicles 28:9—"For the Lord searcheth all hearts, and understandeth all the imaginations of the thoughts."

4. Jeremiah 17:10—"I, the Lord, search the heart."

5. Ezekiel 11:5—"For I know the things that come into your mind, every one of them."

   God knows everything, and Jesus knew that the scribes and Pharisees were thinking evil in their hearts, even to the extent of later wanting to kill Him (Matt. 12:14). An evil heart is one that plots against God, trying to deceive Him. For example, when Ananias and Sapphira tried to deceive God in Acts 5, Peter said, "Why hath Satan filled thine heart to lie to the Holy Spirit?" (v. 3). In Acts 8:20-22, Simon Magus tried to use the gift of God for his own wicked ends. Indicting the scribes and Pharisees for thinking evil in their hearts, Jesus exposed their hypocrisy with a clever argument.

B. Dual Perspective (v. 5)

"For which is easier, to say, Thy sins be forgiven thee; or to say, Arise, and walk?"

First let's consider which would be easier from the perspective

1. Of doing

   The scribes and Pharisees couldn't give an answer, because neither of them are easier—both are impossible for men but are possible for God. They couldn't truthfully say either one, let alone do them. But Jesus could say both, because He could do either with the same divine ease. Only God can heal, and only God can forgive. The scribes and the Pharisees were the ones who taught that disease and sickness were a result of sin. If they really thought about it, their own theology told them that the One who could heal diseases could forgive sin and vice versa. So He said, in effect, "Which is easier, to forgive or to heal? If I can do one, then I can do the other. I'm not a blasphemer—I'm God." They were trapped, because they knew Jesus could heal, and they knew that God was capable of both. If Jesus had power over disease, disasters, demons, and death, then He could certainly deal with sin.

2. Of saying

Which one of the two miracles is easier to *say*? It's easier to say, "Thy sins be forgiven," isn't it? If someone walks up to me, I could say, "Your sins are forgiven," but I can't prove whether or not I accomplished that. But if someone rolls up in a wheel chair and I say, "Rise up and walk," it's going to be pretty easy to verify if I can do that or not. Therefore, the latter statement would be more difficult to say. For that reason, Jesus' choice serves as

C. Direct Proof (v. 6)

"But that ye may know that the Son of man hath power on earth to forgive sins (then saith he to the sick of the palsy), Arise, take up thy bed, and go unto thine house."

If all that Jesus said was, "Your sins be forgiven," those watching would have never known that He actually did that. Therefore, by saying, "Rise up and walk," and by healing the paralytic, they would conclude that Jesus had forgiven his sins because the two are inseparably linked. Jesus was demonstrating His healing power as proof of His power to forgive sin, which was the root of the paralytic's problem. Any pretender can claim to forgive sin, and through the centuries some have claimed that they had the power to do so. But Jesus didn't want the people to think that He was making an empty promise, so He accomplished the visible miracle, which proved He had the power to do the invisible one.

V. FORCE (v. 7)

"And he arose, and departed to his house."

Can you imagine that? The paralytic's four friends had their heads through the roof watching, the people were listening, the scribes and Pharisees were unable to respond—nobody had talked but Jesus in that dramatic scene. He had read His opponents' hearts and nailed them to the proverbial wall with His forensic. And then He simply said, "Get up and go home, fella." Immediately, the man got up, rolled up his little bed under his arm, and picked up its wood frame. You better believe that an aisle was instantly created as the man walked out of that place. When he got outside, you can imagine the excitement when he met his four buddies tripping down the stairs! What power they had experienced! Not only did Jesus have the power to heal that man's disease, He had the power to forgive sin—and still does.

VI. FEAR (v. 8)

"But when the multitudes saw it, they marveled [*phobeō,* "to be afraid''], and glorified God, who had given such power unto men.''

A. The Expressed Reverence

1. Explained

I believe that the multitudes knew that God was working through Jesus. I don't think, however, that they understood the fullness of all that the incarnation meant. But they did know God was there and that He had given power to Jesus—and they were afraid. Isn't that the same reaction we've seen all along to the miracles and teachings of Christ? The reaction of fear has several shades of meanings in classical Greek, but the one that is used most in the New Testament is "awe" or "reverence." It is the kind of fear that someone feels in the presence of one who is infinitely superior.

2. Exemplified

For example, it is used to describe the reaction of people when

a) Jesus was seen walking on the water (Matt. 14:26)

b) Jesus stilled the storm (Mark 4:41)

c) Jesus raised the widow's son at Nain (Luke 7:16)

d) Jesus healed the demoniacs at Gerasa (Luke 8:37)

e) An angel of the Lord appeared to Zacharias beside the altar (Luke 1:12)

f) Zacharias recovered his speech (Luke 1:64)

g) The angels sang to the shepherds (Luke 2:9)

h) The angel rolled the stone away before the guards at the tomb (Matt. 28:2, 4)

i) The women had discovered the empty tomb (Matt. 28:8)

j) The people will be faced with the shattering events of the last days (Luke 21:26)

k) The people saw the signs and wonders and felt the power of the early church (Acts 2:43)

l) The people learned of the death of Ananias and Sapphira (Acts 5:5, 11)

m) The demons overcame the Jewish exorcists at Ephesus (Acts 19:16-17)

In each usage, there is the reverential fear of God or the supernatural.

B. The Expected Results

We should in like manner be in awe of Christ. That type of fear should characterize the Christian today as it did the early church. Acts 9:31 says that the church was "walking in the fear of the Lord." It is essential that we be in awe of Christ, not only because we see the response of fear to the power of God demonstrated in the gospels and in Acts, but also because the epistles exhort us to manifest:

1. A chaste life—First Peter 3:2 says that our "chaste conduct [should be] coupled with fear."

2. Holiness—Second Corinthians 7:1 says that we should be "perfecting holiness in the fear of God."

3. True repentance—Second Corinthians 7:10-11 says that fear is an element of true repentance.

4. A godly Christian life—Philippians 2:12 says that we should work out our salvation "with fear and trembling."

5. Mutual ministry, love, and respect—Ephesians 5:21 indicates that submission has its roots in "the fear of God."

6. Powerful evangelism—Second Corinthians 5:11 says, "Knowing, therefore, the terror of the Lord, we persuade men."

7. Discipline in the church—First Timothy 5:20 says that discipline must be done publicly "that others also may fear."

Christian behavior is to come out of the reverential fear of God. The people who witnessed the healing of the paralytic glorified God, and so should we. They were in awe of His presence—that's the right response. I hope you are in awe of Christ.

So Jesus' forgiveness of sin is the greatest message we have to give. I hope you have experienced that forgiveness. Within the crowd, there were those who were forgiven and those who were furious. Christ offers forgiveness, blots out all the past, and washes away all the sins of the past, present, and future. The greatest news you'll ever hear is that forgiveness is available to you.

Focusing on the Facts

1. What is the most essential message that God gives to sinful man (see p. 77)?

2. The second set of miracles shows Jesus' ability over three realms. What are they? Explain each (see pp. 77-78).

3. After leaving Nazareth, where did Jesus reestablish His home? Mention some Scripture verses that discuss that (see p. 78).

4. Whose house did Jesus possibly reside in (see pp. 78-79)?

5. How did the four men demonstrate that they cared for the paralytic? Why was it necessary for them to assist him (see pp. 79-80)?

6. What are some of the ways in which the paralytic was suffering (see p. 80)?

7. Although not all sickness is directly related to sin, what is sickness a graphic demonstration of (see p. 80)?

8. How did the four men demonstrate their faith in Jesus' ability to heal (see p. 80)?

9. How did the paralytic demonstrate the humility of a seeking heart (see p. 81)?

10. Why did the paralytic have nothing to fear when he came to Jesus (see pp. 81-82)?

11. What was the deepest need that Jesus read in the paralytic's heart (see p. 82)?

12. What are some of the things that the Bible says about sin (see pp. 82-83)?

13. What did the scribes and Pharisees fail to acknowledge their need of? What fact did they refuse to accept? Instead, what did they conclude (see p. 84)?

14. Besides blasphemy, what other accusations did the scribes and Pharisees make in Matthew 8 (see p. 84)?

15. Why would it be easier to say, "Thy sins be forgiven thee" (see p. 86)?

16. According to Matthew 9:6, what did Jesus prove by healing the paralytic (see p. 86)?

17. What was the multitudes' reaction to the power of Jesus (see p. 87)?

18. What type of fear is most common in the New Testament (see p. 87)?

19. According to 2 Corinthians 7:1, in what does holy living find its source (see p. 88)?

Pondering the Principles

1. Have you recently been a stretcher-bearer for anyone? In other words, are you leading people to Christ for salvation? Whom do you know at work, in your neighborhood, or in your family that needs the divine forgiveness that Jesus can give? Do any of them seem to be spiritually "paralyzed" and unwilling to come to Jesus on their own? Determine to care for the spiritual well-being of those you know who need Christ, asking God for wisdom on how you and other believers might carry them into the presence of Christ.

2. Meditate on the following verses about God's great forgiveness: Exodus 34:6-7; Psalm 32:1-5; 130:1-4; Isaiah 55:6-7; Micah 7:18-19; Acts 10:43; Ephesians 2:1-7; 4:32; 1 John 1:7-2:2, 12. If your meditation has brought to your mind something you need to ask forgiveness for, do so now. As part of your meditation, take a few moments to thank God for being rich in mercy.

3. Knowing that God searches your heart and knows your every thought, is there any place you can hide from God? Read Psalm 139:1-12. As believers, how should we respond to a God who knows our thoughts? As you willingly submit your thoughts to His guidance and forgiveness, make the last two verses of Psalm 139 your personal prayer.

7
Jesus' Power over Death—
Part 1

Outline

Introduction
A. The Presence of Death
B. The Passing of Death
C. The Power over Death
  1. The statements of Matthew
    a) Matthew 4:23-24
    b) Matthew 8:16-17
    c) Matthew 9:35
    d) Matthew 11:5
  2. The setting of Matthew

Lesson
  I. Jesus Was Accessible
 II. Jesus Was Available
  A. The Request of Jairus
    1. His position
    2. His prostration
    3. His pleading
      a) A deep need
      b) A determined faith
        (1) Compared to the centurion's faith
        (2) Compared to Martha's faith
  B. The Response of Jesus
III. Jesus Was Touchable
  A. A Desperate Search
    1. The interruption
    2. The illness
    3. The intention
  B. A Double Solution
    1. Physical healing
    2. Spiritual healing

Conclusion

Introduction

A. The Presence of Death

Jesus' power over death is an essential messsage, for we are living in a dying world where all of us face the inevitability of death—we are deteriorating humans in a deteriorating world marked by tragedy and sorrow. Since the fall of man in Genesis 3, there has been a curse on the earth, and that curse has sent the earth and all of its inhabitants careening into the never-ending reality of sadness, disaster, pain, sickness, and death. In any given month, it is not unusual for me to interact with many families who are suffering because loved ones are in the process of dying from terminal illnesses. Or they have died because of tragic accidents. That's just a part of what sin has done to this world.

Is it any wonder that Jesus reacted the way He did when He came to the grave of Lazarus? In John 11 we read, "When Jesus, therefore, saw her [i.e., Mary, the sister of Lazarus] weeping, and the Jews also weeping who came with her, he groaned in the spirit, and was troubled" (v. 33). Arriving at the funeral of Lazarus, Jesus witnessed and even experienced the sorrow over death. Lazarus's death wasn't the only thing that troubled Jesus; contemplating the consequences of sin and empathizing with the pain it brought to man caused Him to hurt deeply. Verses 35-38 say, "Jesus wept. Then said the Jews, Behold how he loved him! And some of them said, Could not this man, who opened the eyes of the blind, have caused that even this man should not have died? Jesus, therefore, again groaning in himself, cometh to the grave." Christ hurt deeply because He could see the power and pain of sin.

B. The Passing of Death

It never was God's plan for sin to mar His creation. All things in the world were created for the good of man; but man sinned, allowing sin to enter creation and run it course. However, the Old Testament prophets tell us that God will reverse the curse. And the great hope at the end of Revelation is that "God shall wipe away all tears from their eyes; and there shall be no death, neither sorrow, nor crying, neither shall there be any more pain; for the former things are passed away" (21:4). John had an incredible vision of the day when the curse is over. But who can reverse the curse and destroy disease, pain, sorrow, and death? The prophets said there would come a Messiah who would have the power to bring back wholeness to life.

C. The Power over Death

When Jesus came into the world, He demonstrated that power. Although the fulfillment of those prophecies is yet future, the One who will fulfill them has sufficiently demonstrated His ability to do so by virtually banishing disease from Palestine, raising the dead, and forgiving sin. All of the things that will be true of the glorious coming kingdom, Jesus demonstrated at His first coming. The miracles of

Jesus verified His power to reverse the curse and establish the kingdom. If He claimed to be the Son of man who would execute judgment upon all and raise the dead (John 5:25-29), then He would have to demonstrate that He had the power to do that.

1. The statements of Matthew

    Matthew shows that the healing power of Jesus is a tremendously important verification of His identity as the Messiah.

    a) Matthew 4:23-24—"And Jesus went about all Galilee, teaching in their synagogues, and preaching the gospel of the kingdom, and healing all manner of sickness and all manner of disease among the people. And his fame went throughout all Syria; and they brought unto him all sick people that were taken with diverse diseases and torments, and those who were possessed with demons, and those who were epileptics, and those who had the palsy; and he healed them."

    b) Matthew 8:16-17—"When the evening was come, they brought unto him many that were possessed with demons; and he cast out the spirits with his word, and healed all that were sick, that it might be fulfilled which was spoken by Isaiah, the prophet." Jesus did not heal people because they had faith or because they were worthy—He healed them in order that He might show that there was no limit to His ability to heal disease.

    c) Matthew 9:35—"And Jesus went about all the cities and villages, teaching in their synagogues, and preaching the gospel of the kingdom, and healing every sickness and every disease among the people."

    d) Matthew 11:5—"The blind receive their sight, and the lame walk, the lepers are cleansed, and the deaf hear, the dead are raised up, and the poor have the gospel preached to them."

    So it was that Jesus demonstrated that He was God's Messiah, the King of creation.

2. The setting of Matthew

    Through chapters 8 and 9 of Matthew, we see three groups with three miracles each. The first group of miracles, in 8:2-15, deals with disease. The second group, from 8:23—9:17, deals with disorder in the physical, spiritual, and moral realms. The third group, in 9:18-34, deals with death and serves as a climax. The last group also includes the miracles of giving sight to the blind and speech to the dumb, which may seem less marvelous than resurrection, but nevertheless are related illustrations of Jesus' resurrection power. First He raises the whole person from the dead, and then He shows that He can raise the whole by giving life to dead parts. He who gave sight to dead eyes and speech to a dead tongue can also raise the dead, for that is only the sum of the parts.

    Can Jesus overcome death? G. B. Hardy, a Canadian scientist, was led to consider that question in his book *Countdown: A Time to Choose* (Chicago: Moody, 1971). In his examination of religion, he sought to find if anyone had ever conquered death, and if someone had, whether or not he had made a way for him to conquer it too. Upon examining the tombs of several religious leaders, he learned that they were still occupied. But when he came to the tomb of Jesus, he learned that it was empty. He also discovered that Jesus had said, "Because I live, ye shall live also" (John 14:19). Hardy concluded that there was One who could conquer death and open the way for him to follow. Clearly Jesus is the One who is able to reverse the curse of death, for He holds in His hands the keys of death and hell (Rev. 1:18). The Jesus who stood at the grave of Lazarus and wept with Mary was the same One who said to Martha, "I am the resurrection, and the life; he that believeth in me, though he were dead, yet shall he live. And whosoever liveth and believeth in me shall never die. Believest thou this?" (John 11:25-26).

Jesus' power over death is clearly demonstrated in Matthew 9 with the raising of a girl who had died. However, prior to that miracle, He healed a woman with an issue of blood. That healing is really part of the resurrection miracle, for it provided the delay that was necessary for the girl's death to occur, making the resurrection as dramatic as possible. As we examine those miracles, I want you to see the power of Christ but at the same time note how Jesus dealt with others. Nowhere is the tenderness and sensitivity of Jesus more wonderfully seen against the background of His power and majesty than here. This marvelous glimpse of how Jesus dealt with people even becomes a pattern for us in dealing with others too. For that reason, I am going to use an outline based upon how Jesus dealt with people to lead us through this tremendous account.

Lesson

I. JESUS WAS ACCESSIBLE (v. 18*a*)

"While he spoke these things unto them, behold, there came a certain ruler."

What was Jesus speaking about and to whom? Do you remember what was going on here? Jesus had cast the demons out of the demoniacs of Gadara and sent them into a herd of swine. He had calmed the sea and wind. When He came back to Capernaum, He returned to the house where Peter lived. And the disciples of John the Baptist came and said, "Why aren't your disciples fasting like we and the Pharisees are?" (Matt. 9:14).

Now, as Jesus was interacting with the Pharisees and the disciples of John the Baptist, a certain ruler came to Him. That speaks to me of Jesus' accessibility. He was not some religious guru in an ivory tower with lilies all around Him. He didn't live in a monastery. People didn't have to work their way up a hierarchy before they could have an audience with Him. Rather, He moved among common people. As God come to earth, Jesus pitched His tent with men, according to the literal Greek rendering of John 1:14. He was in the streets of the villages; He walked the dusty roads; He was in the synagogues; He was in the homes of others.

One day a lot of parents came to Him and brought their little children. When the disciples said, "Send those kids away," Jesus said, "Permit little children . . . to come unto me; for of such is the kingdom" (Matt. 19:14), and He gathered the little ones to Himself. Jesus was accessible to adults and to little children as well. Almost everywhere He went He moved in a crowd. On another occasion He said, "I have compassion on the multitude, because they continue with me now three days" (Matt. 15:32). And do you think people asked Him questions when they got next to Him? Wouldn't you? Don't you think they brought Him all their problems? He was One who had all the answers. He was counseling, healing, and teaching in the midst of the people for three solid days. He even had to retreat to the Mount of Olives on occasion to commune with the Father in solitude. There were times when it was necessary for Him to tell others not to spread the news about His miracles because of the increased pressure that would result.

There was Jesus—the Creator of the universe, King of kings and Lord of lords—walking around the rolling hills of Galilee, with little children running near Him and people stopping Him and talking. Whether He was in the villages, in a boat on the water, or even in the crowded streets of Jerusalem, He was nearly always surrounded by people. That tells me that God is accessible, because Jesus was God displaying Himself.

At that particular time, two people were in the crowd—one was a ruler, the other, a sick lady. One was respected and well off, the other was definitely down-and-out. Can you imagine the assortment of people that would have been in a crowd like that? There would have been Pharisees who were trying to condemn Him, people who were trying to analyze Him, and people who were sick, hurting, poor, and downcast, trying to have their needs met. It thrills me to see how accessible Jesus was to the crowds.

II. JESUS WAS AVAILABLE (vv. 18b-19)

Jesus was not only accessible in that you could get to Him; He was available in that He would come to you. It's a marvelous reality that Jesus would respond to a particular person by being available.

A. The Request of Jairus (v. 18b-d)

1. His position (v. 18b)

   "Behold, there came a certain ruler."

   The word "behold" tells us that this was a remarkable incident. According to Mark and Luke, Jairus was one of the rulers of the synagogue and possibly even the chief elder. If so, he was the number-one representative of the religious establishment in Capernaum. Synagogues were ruled by elders who served as spiritual leaders. They were also responsible for the administration of the synagogue and coordinating the public worship. As men of great influence, the elders would appoint from among themselves a presiding ruler, who in turn would appoint those who were to preach, pray, and read out of the law. This ruler was responsible for administrating the entire operation of the synagogue. He was a member of the religious establishment that, for the most part, was set against Christ, fighting Him tooth and nail throughout His ministry. Consequently, Jairus would have had a lot of peer pressure to be a faithful Jewish religionist. For that reason, as he came to Jesus, you might have expected him to say, "Sir, I am the chief elder of the synagogue; I'd like to speak to You. Could we please have a private conversation?" But that's not what he said. He was not concerned about protecting his reputation.

2. His prostration (v. 18c)

"And worshiped him."

The word "worship" in ancient Greek describes a person who prostrated himself before another, often kissing the other person's feet, the hem of his garment, or the ground in front of him as an expression of respect. It is amazing, therefore, that this word is used to describe the action of an official from the religious establishment, for such reverence was only offered to a deity, a supernatural being, something considered holy, or a king who was considered to be divine. Using the word thirteen times in his gospel, Matthew shows that it is a fitting response to the King. But what would have made that ruler bow down before Jesus?

3. His pleading (v. 18d)

"Saying, My daughter is even now dead; but come and lay thy hand upon her, and she shall live."

The accounts of Mark and Luke fill in more details, telling us that when the ruler initially spoke to Jesus, his daughter was in the process of dying. But Matthew condenses it all, reporting that she had died. Do you know why Jairus came to Jesus? He didn't care about the social pressure of the religious establishment—his daughter was dead, and there were no resources within his system to deal with that. I believe that God had already been working in his heart, because his faith expressed not a taint of doubt. He knew that when Jesus touched his daughter, she would live. He swallowed his pride, turned his back on social pressure, and said good-bye to the religious establishment, as he fell flat on his face before Jesus. Let me give you two reasons that he was willing to do this.

a) A deep need

That is why people come to Christ. If you don't recognize your need for Him, you are not going to come. I once had a man say to me, "I have no need of Christ." I replied, "If you don't have any need of Christ, then you're not going to come to Him. We should pray that you would know pain, desperation, or the loss of all your resources so that you would recognize your need of Christ and come to Him." It's apparent to me that the man probably believed in the power of Christ, but maybe until that point, he had been somewhat hesitant to express that belief. However, now that his daughter was dying, he came in desperation. Evidently his motive wasn't totally pure—he didn't come just because of his love for Jesus; he came because he was hurting deeply from emotional pain. His heart was crushed with grief. It's the people with a need that come to Christ. That is why the gospel is so often received by the poor, the sick, the weak, and the prisoners.

b) A determined faith

Even though his faith was inadequate and his motive was a little bit selfish, Jesus was still available to him. He really did believe that Jesus had the power to heal her and even raise her from the dead. That is a marvelous expression of faith rarely surpassed in the gospels.

(1) Compared to the centurion's faith

In Matthew 8, a centurion whose servant was afflicted with paralysis said, "Speak the word only, and my servant shall be healed. . . . When Jesus heard it, he marveled, and said to them that followed, Verily I say unto you, I have not found so great faith, no, not in Israel" (vv. 8*b*, 10). That man had enough faith to believe that Jesus could heal his servant with a word. If that was the greatest example of faith He'd seen in Israel, then what kind of faith was that which believed Jesus could raise a dead person to life? The faith of the synagogue official may have even surpassed that of the centurion.

(2) Compared to Martha's faith

Martha said to Jesus, "If You had only been here when my brother was sick, You could have done something; now he's dead and it's too late" (John 11:21). She had her doubts about the resurrection power of Jesus.

I believe that the synagogue official had the faith to be redeemed. Before the day was over, he had entered into the kingdom of God. How did Jesus respond to his need and his faith?

B. The Response of Jesus (v. 19)

"And Jesus arose, and followed him, and so did his disciples."

Jesus didn't say, "Well, I've got this very important meeting here with the multitude and I don't know how I'm going to have a chance to slip away, because there are lots of sick people that need Me here." He rose up and followed him. There are times when there are tremendous needs in an individual's life, and Jesus is always sensitive to that. John 6:37 says, "Him that cometh to me I will in no wise cast out."

III. JESUS WAS TOUCHABLE (vv. 20-22)

A. A Desperate Search (vv. 20-21)

After Jesus had left to go with Jairus, being followed by His disciples and the multitude, there came a woman desperately searching to be healed. "And, behold, a woman, who had been diseased with an issue of blood twelve years, came behind him, and touched the hem of his garment" (v. 20).

1. The interruption

In that culture, a woman wouldn't go around touching men, let alone grabbing them, as the word "touch" indicates in the Greek. The same word is used in John 20 when Mary was clinging to Jesus after finding that He had risen from the dead. In effect, He said, "You can't hang onto Me; I've got to go back to heaven and send the Holy Spirit—you can't keep Me here." Similarly, that woman reached out and grabbed on to Jesus' garment in desperation, having been diseased with an issue of blood for twelve years.

2. The illness

What type of illness was this issue of blood? For twelve years the woman could not stop bleeding. Its cause was due, perhaps, to a fibroid tumor in the uterus, something that would be readily treated today by surgery. As a result of her condition, she was considered perpetually unclean. Luke said that she could not be cured (8:43), and Mark said that she had spent all her money on doctors and was even worse (5:26).

From the Jewish point of view, you couldn't imagine anything worse than being a woman with an issue of blood. It was humiliating beyond anything else, with the possible exception of leprosy. The disease rendered the sufferer unclean, according to Leviticus 15:25-27, "And if a woman have an issue of her blood many days out of the time of her separation, or if it run beyond the time of her separation, all the days of the issue of her uncleanness shall be as the days of her separation: she shall be unclean. Every bed whereon she lieth all the days of her issue shall be unto her as the bed of her separation; and whatsoever she sitteth upon shall be unclean, as the uncleanness of her separation. And whosoever toucheth those things shall be unclean, and shall wash his clothes and bathe himself in water, and be unclean until the evening." Leviticus says that a woman with an issue of blood was ceremonially unclean. Every bed she laid upon and everything she sat on, anything she wore, and anyone who touched her also became unclean. Therefore, she was excommunicated from the synagogue, divorced by her husband, and ostracized from all human relationships. Consequently, for twelve years that poor woman had lived in isolation.

Do you see why she so desperately sought to touch Jesus? She too had a deep need and believed in Him. She had lost all sense of propriety in her desperation. Some people say, "I'd like to come to Christ, but I'm certainly not going to openly walk into the church's counseling room." They aren't desperate enough. But if they ever get to the point of true desperation, they would probably knock the door of the counseling room down if it weren't open.

3. The intention

The woman touched the hem (Gk., *kraspedon,* "tassel"; Heb., *zizith,* "fringe") of Jesus' garment. In the Old Testament (Num. 15:37-41; Deut. 22:12), the Israelites were instructed to mark their garments with a fringe of four blue tassels symbolizing the law of God. They identified a Jewish person as a member of God's chosen people regardless of where he was in the world and reminded him every time he took his clothes off or put them on that he belonged to God. We have similar reminders today—some people wear a cross or fish symbol.

The tassels on Christ's clothing probably swung a little bit as He moved through the crowd. Reaching out for one of them, the woman kept saying to herself, "If I may but touch his garment, I shall be well" (Matt. 9:21*b*). And as she struggled through the crowd and finally grabbed the tassel, there came

B. A Double Solution (v. 22)

1. Physical healing

Instantly she was healed. Mark says that when the Lord felt power involuntarily pass from Him, He said, "Who touched my clothes?" (5:30*b*). When the woman grabbed the tassel, Jesus suddenly stopped in the midst of the crowd; it was as if time itself stopped, and for the moment it seemed as if only the woman and her great need existed. The disciples didn't understand Jesus' sensitivity to a seeking heart. Mark 5:31 and Luke 8:45 record them as saying, in effect, "Are You kidding? How can You say, 'Who touched Me?' People are crowding all around You."

When Jesus looked around, He found the woman who had faith that He could heal her. Granted, her faith was not a mature faith, for it was somewhat superstitious. But the Lord responded to it anyway. Even faith as small as a mustard seed will move a mountain. The Lord can take an inadequate faith like Jairus's, which was somewhat selfish, and a superstitious faith, like that woman's, and create saving faith.

2. Spiritual healing

Jesus couldn't just let that lady go, or maybe she would have concluded that superstition was effective. He pulled her into the fullness of a relationship with Him. I don't really believe she was healed by her faith; I think she was healed by the sovereignty of God—He choose to heal her. Faith wasn't always present in the people Jesus healed. When Jesus said, "Thy faith hath made thee well" (9:22), He didn't use the usual word for healing, *iaomai;*

98

He used *sōzō*, which can mean to save in terms of redemption. Jesus did miracles of healing everywhere, even for those who had no faith, but He saved only those who had faith in Him. For that reason, I think there was a redemptive element in her faith. Rather than leaving her superstitious about His healing power, Jesus drew her out and saved her.

The ruler had an inadequate motive of selfishness, the woman had an inadequate faith involving superstition, and yet Jesus redeemed them both. Their faith was like that of the man who said, "Lord, I believe; help thou mine unbelief" (Mark 9:24). In other words, "Take me where I am with my little faith and move me to saving faith." Jesus always knew the difference between the jostling of the fickle mob and the grasping of the faithful soul.

Conclusion

Jesus is accessible, available, and touchable. But there are only two things that will bring you to Him. The first is a deep need, a sense of desperation over your condition, and the second is great faith. Do you believe in Christ? Have you looked at your life and seen that it is less than what it ought to be? Do you want to reach out and see somebody transform it? Consider these prayerful words:

> Like her, dear Lord, I too would come:
> Sick, sin stained, amid the crowd alone.
> I dare not tell to all their ears
> The longings which are to Thee known.
>
> Help, help gracious Lord, no eye but Thine
> Can graze the hills of bygone years,
> All human aid is vain but Thou
> Canst heal my wounds and dry my tears.
>
> Oh God, if only I may touch
> Thy saving virtue soul to soul,
> Then come what may let all men know
> That Jesus Christ has made me whole.
>
> (Author Unknown)

Jesus is touchable, available, and accessible. He is God, operating in the world of man through His Spirit, and He is able to transform your life.

Focusing on the Facts

1. Why is Jesus' power over death an essential message for us (see p. 91)?
2. What two things troubled Jesus at the tomb of Lazarus (see p. 91)?
3. Although the curse of sin has marred God's perfect creation, what hope does the Bible offer for the future (see p. 91)?
4. What does Matthew show us as an important verification of Jesus' identity as the Messiah (see p. 92)?
5. What is the primary reason that Jesus healed people? Were faith and worthiness required in an individual's life for Him to do so (see p. 92)?

6. How are the healings of the blind and the dumb in the third set of miracles related illustrations of Jesus' resurrection power (see p. 92)?

7. What two questions did G. B. Hardy ask in his examination of religion, and what two answers did he find (see p. 93)?

8. Against the background of Jesus' power and majesty, what do we see about Christ's dealings with people in Matthew 9:18-22 (see p. 93)?

9. In what ways was Jesus accessible (see pp. 93-94)?

10. How did Jesus demonstrate His availability to the individual (see p. 94)?

11. Why is it remarkable that the ruler of Matthew 9:18 would come to Jesus for help (see pp. 94-95)?

12. What made that ruler come and bow down before Jesus (see p. 95)?

13. How was Jesus interrupted as He went to help Jairus? What did the interruption become for Jesus (see pp. 97-99)?

14. Why was the woman's condition so desperate (see p. 97)?

15. How did the Lord respond to the woman's somewhat superstitious faith (see p. 98)?

16. As implied by the Greek verb, what other type of healing did the woman receive (see p. 99)?

17. What are two elements that will bring a person to Christ (see p. 99)?

Pondering the Principles

1. Think back to the two questions G. B. Hardy asked when examining religion (see p. 93). Do you think those are questions all men desire to know the answers to even though they may have never consciously asked them? Assuming that eternal life is something that all men seek, what truths could you relate to people that might lead them to consider Jesus? Memorize Jesus' claim to be "the resurrection, and the life" in John 11:25-26, being ready to share it when the topics of death and life after death are being discussed.

2. Meditate on Philippians 2:5-8 and Hebrews 4:14-16. Thank God that He loved man enough to make Himself accessible by coming to earth in the person of Jesus, humbling Himself and dying on the cross for our sake, and offering mercy and grace to us in time of need as a sympathetic Savior.

3. Is there a sense of desperation in your life because of a physical, emotional, or spiritual problem? If you have recognized your deep need, do you believe that Jesus Christ can meet it? Are you willing to fall into the loving arms of Jesus in spite of the often skeptical and ridiculing eyes of the world? If so, your humble faith will be rewarded, according to 1 Peter 5:6-7.

8
Jesus' Power over Death— Part 2

Outline

Introduction
A. The Peril of Death
B. The Power over Death
   1. John 5:21, 24, 26
   2. John 11:25-26
   3. John 14:19
   4. 1 Corinthians 15:54-57
   5. Revelation 21:4
   6. Matthew 11:3-5

Review
I. Jesus Was Accessible
II. Jesus Was Available
   A. The Request of Jairus
      1. His position
      2. His prostration
         a) The disciples in the boat
         b) The woman of Syrophoenicia
      3. His pleading
   B. The Response of Jesus
III. Jesus Was Touchable
   A. A Desperate Search
   B. A Double Solution
      1. Physical healing
      2. Spiritual healing

Lesson
      a) Mark 10:46-52
      b) Luke 7:44-50
      c) Luke 17:14-19
IV. Jesus Was Impartial
   A. The Standard of Choice
   B. The Sovereignty of Choice
      1. Considered
      2. Contrasted

V. Jesus Was Powerful
  A. The Ranting
     1. The rending of garments
     2. The wailing for the dead
     3. The playing of flutes
  B. The Ridicule
  C. The Resurrection
  D. The Result

Conclusion

Introduction

A. The Peril of Death

Nothing is more wonderful than to know that Christ has conquered death. The writer of Hebrews tell us that Jesus came to "destroy him that had the power of death, that is, the devil, and deliver them who, through fear of death, were all their lifetime subject to bondage" (2:14b-15). In other words, he says that men live their entire lives subject to the fear of death, but Christ has come to deliver them from that fear.

Death is the specter that haunts every person's life—the longer you live, the more inevitably it looms in the future. To know that Christ has conquered death, however, is the ultimate joy. Yet, for most of the world, there is no such knowledge, and therefore men fear death. I suppose the man who seemed to be at peace in my lifetime was Mahatma Gandhi. He seemed to have absolute tranquility of soul, knowing nothing of fear. Fifteen years before his death, Gandhi wrote, "I must tell you in all humility that Hinduism, as I know it, entirely satisfies my soul, fills my whole being, and I find a solace in the Bhagavad and Upanishads that I miss even in the Sermon on the Mount." Then, just before his death he wrote this: "My days are numbered. I am not likely to live very long—perhaps a year or a little more. For the first time in fifty years I find myself in the slough of despond. [Evidently, he must have been reading the Christian classic *Pilgrim's Progress.*] All about me is darkness; I am praying for light." Even Mahatma Gandhi, who seemed to have his life in order, saw his confidence falling apart as he began to face the inevitability of death.

B. The Power over Death

Death looms on the horizon of every individual's life. How marvelous it is to realize, then, that Jesus came to conquer death.

  1. John 5:21, 24, 26—"For as the Father raiseth up the dead, and giveth them life, even so the Son giveth life to whom he will. . . . Verily, verily, I say unto you, He that heareth my word, and believeth on him that sent me, hath everlasting life. . . . For as the Father hath life in himself, so hath he given to the Son to have life in himself."

102

2. John 11:25-26—"I am the resurrection, and the life; he that believeth in me, though he were dead, yet shall he live. And whosoever liveth and believeth in me shall never die." In other words, Jesus claimed to have power over death.

3. John 14:19—"Because I live, ye shall live also."

4. 1 Corinthians 15:54-57—The work of the Messiah was to conquer death. The apostle Paul said that the resurrection of Christ took the sting out of death, giving victory over the grave.

5. Revelation 21:4—Ultimately, the Messiah would bring about an eternal state where "there shall be no more death."

6. Matthew 11:3-5—As the Messiah, Jesus was demonstrating His power over disease, disablement, and death. John the Baptist was concerned to know if Jesus was truly the Messiah. Therefore he sent a couple of disciples to find out: "Art thou he that should come, or do we look for another? Jesus answered and said unto them, Go and show John again those things which ye do hear and see: The blind receive their sight, and the lame walk, the lepers are cleansed, and the deaf hear, the dead are raised up." Those credentials help us to know that He is the King.

Review

Wanting us to understand that Jesus is the Messiah, in chapters 8 and 9 Matthew presents the miraculous power of Jesus over disease, disorder, and death. Besides seeing His power, we also learn how Jesus dealt with people.

I. JESUS WAS ACCESSIBLE (v. 18a; see pp. 93-94)

Everywhere Jesus went, there was a mass of humanity crowding around Him. We see Him surrounded by people throughout the book of Matthew, as the following phrases show: "And there followed him great multitudes of people" (4:25a); "when he was come down from the mountain, great multitudes followed him" (8:1; cf. 12:15; 19:2; 20:29; 21:8). In other words, Jesus was accessible to people who came with questions to be answered and needs to be met.

II. JESUS WAS AVAILABLE (vv. 18b-19; see pp. 94-96)

In the midst of the crowd, Jesus focused upon a man and a woman. He was not only accessible so that you could attend His meetings; He was also available so that you could face Him individually. He responded to individual people. He touched a leper, He went to the home of a centurion who had a paralyzed servant, He touched a woman with a fever, He cast demons out of some men, He healed a paralytic, and He responded to

A. The Request of Jairus (v. 18b; see pp. 94-96)

1. His position (see pp. 94-95)

A ruler of the synagogue came to Jesus with a great need. His daughter was at the point of death. He also expressed great faith in that he believed Jesus could bring her back to life.

2. His prostration (see p. 95)

The ruler demonstrated his saving faith by worshiping Jesus. Although worship can be hypocritical (Matt. 18:26) and self-seeking (Matt. 20:20), it can also be genuine.

a) The disciples in the boat

After Jesus had walked on the water and calmed the wind, "then they that were in the boat came and worshiped him, saying, Of a truth, thou art the Son of God" (Matt. 14:33).

b) The woman of Syrophoenicia

We can also see true worship in Matthew 15:21-28: "Then Jesus went from there, and departed into the borders of Tyre and Sidon. And, behold, a woman of Canaan came out of the same borders, and cried unto him, saying, Have mercy on me, O Lord, thou Son of David; my daughter is grievously vexed with a demon. But he answered her not a word. And his disciples came and besought him, saying, Send her away; for she crieth after us. But he answered and said, I am not sent but unto the lost sheep of the house of Israel. [Jesus was explaining that the priority of His ministry was to offer the kingdom to the Jewish people.] Then came she and worshiped him, saying, Lord, help me. But he answered and said, It is not right to take the children's bread, and to cast it to dogs. And she said, Truth, Lord; yet the dogs eat the crumbs which fall from their master's table. Then Jesus answered and said unto her, O woman, great is thy faith." She knew as a Gentile that she didn't deserve the messianic blessings meant for Israel. Her persevering faith adorned the true worship she offered to Jesus.

3. His pleading (see pp. 95-96)

Similarly, I believe that the ruler of the synagogue offered Jesus real worship, believing that He could heal and even raise the dead. Such faith was greater than that of the disciples, who were rebuked a few times for having "little faith" (Matt. 6:30; 8:26; 14:31; 16:8). If the disciples had little faith, but were saved in spite of it, then certainly the ruler's greater faith must have been adequate for redemption. He had a deep need and great faith.

B. The Response of Jesus (v. 19; see p. 96)

III. JESUS WAS TOUCHABLE (vv. 20-22; see pp. 97-99)

A. A Desperate Search (vv. 20-21; see pp. 97-98)

A woman, who had been declared unclean by Levitical law, had been ostracized from society because of an illness she had suffered from for twelve years. She sought healing by touching the tassels of Jesus' garment as He walked with the crowd to Jairus's house.

B. A Double Solution (v. 22; see pp. 98-99)

1. Physical healing (see p. 98)

She came with the humility that was later exemplified by James Simpson. When he lay dying, a friend wished to comfort him and said, "James, soon you will be able to rest on the bosom of Jesus." "Well, I don't know that I can quite do that," Simpson replied, "but I do think I have got hold on the hem of His garment." Not wanting to be exposed in her embarrassment and shame, the woman reached out to touch Jesus in the jostling crowd and was immediately healed (Luke 8:44). And Jesus, sensitive enough to know the difference between the jostling of the fickle mob and the grasping of a faithful soul, perceived that power had gone out from Him (Luke 8:46). That tells me that Jesus was so much a channel of the Father's will, that the Father could heal through Him before He even knew who was being healed. He had come to do the will of Him who had sent Him (John 5:30). His intense sensitivity allowed Him to discern between the thrill seekers who pressed against Him out of curiosity and people who hung on in desperation and faith.

Jesus responded to the woman's seeking heart by granting her

2. Spiritual healing (see pp. 98-99)

In addition to the woman's physical healing, Jesus, in effect, pulled her out of the crowd and said, "There's something else. Your healing didn't have anything to do with your faith—that was a sovereign act of God. However, your faith has saved you." She was saved from the horrors of her disease, but the use of the Greek word *sōzō* implies that there was also a redemptive issue involved.

Completing our review, let us consider the redemptive element in being "made well."

Lesson

a) Mark 10:46-52

"And they came to Jericho; and as he went out of Jericho with his disciples and a great number of people, blind Bartimaeus, the son of Timaeus, sat by the wayside begging. And when he heard that it was Jesus of Nazareth, he began to cry out, and say, Jesus, thou Son of David; have mercy on me. And many charged him that he should hold his peace; but he cried the more, a great deal, Thou Son of David; have mercy on me. And Jesus stood still, and commanded him to be called. And they call the blind man, saying unto him, Be of good comfort; rise, he calleth thee. And he, casting away his garment, rose and came to Jesus. And Jesus answered and said unto him, What wilt thou that I should do unto thee? The blind man said unto him, Lord, that I might receive my sight. And Jesus said unto him, Go thy way; thy faith hath made thee well [lit., "saved thee"; Gk., *sōzō*]. And immediately he received his sight, and followed Jesus on the way." I think in that case the word *sōzō* indicates that the man not only was healed, but he also received salvation. He had the kind of faith that was sufficient to save his soul. He believed that Jesus was the Lord, the Son of David (a messianic title).

b) Luke 7:44-50

"And he turned to the woman, and said unto Simon, Seest thou this woman? I entered into thine house; thou gavest me no water for my feet. But she hath washed my feet with tears, and wiped them with the hair of her head. Thou gavest me no kiss. But this woman, since the time I came in, hath not ceased to kiss my feet. My head with oil thou didst not anoint. But this woman hath anointed my feet with ointment. Wherefore, I say unto thee, Her sins, which are many, are forgiven; for she loved much. But to whom little is forgiven, the same loveth little. And he said unto her, Thy sins are forgiven. [The woman demonstrated so much love and respect for Christ that He redeemed her by forgiving her sin.] And they that were eating with him began to say within themselves, Who is this that forgiveth sins also? And he said to the woman, Thy faith hath saved thee; go in peace." The latter phrase uses the same verb, *sōzō*, used in the previous passages. However, no healing occurred in this last passage—only the forgiveness of sin. That is why the phrase, which clearly speaks of the woman's salvation, also speaks of the salvation that accompanied the healings of other people.

c) Luke 17:14-19

Ten lepers came to Jesus "as he went to Jerusalem" (v. 11). "And when he saw them, he said unto them, Go show yourselves unto the priests. And it came to pass that, as they went, they were cleansed [Gk., *katharizō*, "to be washed, cleansed"]. And one of them, when he saw that he was healed, turned back, and with a loud voice glorified God, and fell down on his face at his feet, giving him thanks; and he was a Samaritan. And Jesus, answering, said, Were there not ten cleansed? But where are the nine? There are not found that returned to give glory to God, except this stranger. And he said unto him, Arise, go thy way; thy faith hath made thee well [or, "saved thee"; Gk., *sōzō*]." It's one thing to be cleansed (*katharizō*); it's something else to be saved (*sōzō*). There was a healing of ten, but only one was saved.

I believe that when *sōzō* is used in a healing context, it implies a redemptive aspect, because we know that faith is not necessary for healing. There are many non-Christians who have diseases but still get well, and there are Christians who die. Sometimes God honors our faith by healing, but He always honors our faith by saving us.

106

IV. JESUS WAS IMPARTIAL (v. 22a)

"But Jesus turned about, and when he saw her, he said, Daughter, be of good comfort."

A. The Standard of Choice

When Jesus turned around to face that woman, He showed that He was impartial. He could have said, "Look, lady, could you let go of My tassel? I'm trying to get to the ruler's house. If we can get this guy who runs the synagogue converted, we can have a revival in this town. So please let go; I have something very important to attend to." No, God has never looked for the superstars and the famous people; He's always been content with simple folk. The Bible says that the prophet Isaiah predicted when the Messiah would come, He would preach the gospel to the poor (61:1). Paul said that "not many wise men after the flesh, not many mighty, not many noble, are called; but God hath chosen the foolish things . . . the weak things . . . and base things . . . and things which are despised" (1 Cor. 1:26-28). Christians constitute a motley crew.

B. The Sovereignty of Choice

1. Considered

I was reading a very interesting book called *Fearfully and Wonderfully Made* written by Dr. Paul Brand and Philip Yancey. In it they talk about how the people of God are such an unlikely bunch to be saved. They quote from novelist Frederick Buechner, who said:

> Who could have predicted that God would choose not Esau, the honest and reliable, but Jacob, the trickster and heel, that he would put his finger on Noah, who hit the bottle, or on Moses, who was trying to beat the rap in Midian for braining a man in Egypt and said if it weren't for the honor of the thing he'd just as soon let Aaron go back and face the music, or on the prophets who were a ragged lot, mad as hatters most of them . . . ?

And then Dr. Brand adds:

> The exception seems to be the rule. The first humans God created went out and did the only thing God asked them not to do. The man He chose to head a new nation known as "God's people" tried to pawn off his wife on an unsuspecting Pharaoh. And the wife herself, when told at the ripe old age of ninety-one that God was ready to deliver the son He had promised her, broke into rasping laughter in the face of God. Rahab, a harlot, became revered for her great faith. And Solomon, the wisest man who ever lived, went out of his way to break every proverb he so astutely composed.

> Even after Jesus came the pattern continued. The two disciples who did the most to spread the word after His departure, John and Peter, were the two He had rebuked most often for petty squabbling and muddle-headedness. And the apostle Paul, who wrote more books than any other Bible writer, was selected for the task while kicking up dust whirls from town to town sniffing out Christians to torture. Jesus had

nerve, entrusting the high-minded ideals of love and unity and fellow-ship to this group. No wonder cynics have looked at the church and sighed, "If that group of people is supposed to represent God, I'll quickly vote against Him." Or, as Nietzsche expressed it, "His disciples will have to look more saved if I am to believe in their savior."*

We are a motley crew, aren't we? But we all have this in common: We have a sense of desperate need, and we have faith to believe in Christ. Even though Jesus was on His way with the ruler, He impartially stopped to bring salvation to an outcast. As Peter said, "God is no respecter of persons" (Acts 10:34). Paul adds that in God's eyes, "there is neither Jew nor Greek, there is neither bond nor free, there is neither male nor female; for ye are all one in Christ Jesus" (Gal. 3:28). Jesus dealt with the woman not from a distance, but in an intimate and tender way, saying, "Daughter, be of good comfort" (v. 22). What impartiality! It's clear that Jesus loved people. A little outcast lady was as important to Him as the ruler of a synagogue. May God deliver us from playing up to the "respected" people and ignoring the needy.

2. Contrasted

In the book *A Night to Remember,* Walter Lord tells about the sinking of the *Titanic* in 1912. When the tragedy was published in *The American,* a New York newspaper, the article focused almost entirely upon John Jacob Astor, a millionaire who had drowned. Eighteen hundred other people also drowned, but typically, the world is only interested in the rich and famous. Not so with Christ. If you learn anything from our passage in Matthew, learn not only how powerful Jesus is, but also how accessible, available, touchable, and impartial He is. That's how it is with God, and that's how it should be with those who represent Him.

V. JESUS WAS POWERFUL (vv. 23-26)

We can express the first four characteristics of Christ, but that is where it stops for us. I can sympathize with you and hold out my hand to help you, but if you're sick, I can't heal you. If you're dead, I can't raise you. Christ's power sets Him apart from all others. Let's examine the passage depicting Jesus' power.

A. The Ranting (v. 23)

"And when Jesus came into the ruler's house, and saw the musicians and the people making a noise."

By the time Jesus had arrived at the house, the girl was dead and a funeral service was in progress. The noisy racket was quite different from what we are used to in a funeral home within our culture. Three basic things went on at a Jewish funeral.

*Taken from *Fearfully and Wonderfully Made* [pp. 29-30], by Dr. Paul Brand and Philip Yancey. Copyright © 1980 by Dr. Paul Brand and Philip Yancey. Used by permission of Zondervan Publishing House.

108

1. The rending of garments

   Ripping one's clothes was symbolic of one's grief. The Talmud contained thirty-nine different rules and regulations on how to rip your clothes. For example, a person had to do it while he was standing up, over or near his heart. The rip had to be big enough to stick a fist through, and it had to be left seven days. For the next thirty days it could be loosely stitched and then afterwards, sewn permanently. In order that women not expose themselves in an indiscreet manner, they would rip their undergarment, wear it backwards, and then rip their outer garments in public.

2. The wailing for the dead

   Professional wailing women would be sent for and kept in readiness. They would learn the domestic history of the whole family and bring up names of those who had recently died, trying to touch some tender chord in every heart.

3. The playing of flutes

   The third element in Jewish mourning was the use of musicians. The Talmud specifically called for flutes: "The husband is bound to bury his dead wife and to make lamentations and mourning for her according to the custom of all countries. And also the very poorest among the Israelites will not allow her less than two flutes and one wailing woman; but, if he be rich, let all things be done according to his qualities."

   Jairus was probably well off, and his house would be filled with flute players, people ripping their clothes, and mourners wailing incessantly. Flute playing also accompanied mourning in the Roman world. Seneca wrote that there were so many flute players at the funeral of the Emperor Claudius that Claudius himself probably heard them.

B. The Ridicule (v. 24)

   "He said unto them, Give place; for the maid is not dead, but sleepeth. And they laughed him to scorn."

When Jesus saw the musicians and heard the people making all that noise, He said, "Go away. The girl is not dead; she's only sleeping." Some of those present laughed in His face: "What is He saying? He must know that she's dead; it's been reported already. Does He think He is going to raise her from the dead? But Jesus meant that they could not treat her death as a true death—but rather as sleep—because it would be so temporary. The implication was that Jesus would raise her from the dead, and that brought scornful laughter. Such abrupt laughter shows you that those wailing were paid mourners. They could cry for the child or laugh at Jesus in an instant. Their laughter was the hard laughter of mockery, as when a person laughs at someone they consider inferior. That verb is only used in this story by all three synoptic gospel writers. It is the kind of scornful laughter reserved for mocking a fool. In their eyes, only a fool would think he could raise her from the dead. Although the crowd in Capernaum had seen other miracles, they still didn't believe in Christ. But He was well aware of the fact that people who saw His miracles didn't necessarily believe in Him. At another time He said, "If they hear not Moses and the prophets, neither will they be persuaded, though one rose from the dead" (Luke 16:31).

C. The Resurrection (v. 25)

"But when the people were put forth, he went in, and took her by the hand, and the maid arose."

Mark's gospel records that He said to her, "Talitha cumi" (5:41), which means, "Little girl, arise." And when the girl arose, "her parents were amazed; but he charged them that they should tell no man what was done" (Luke 8:56). Evidently they couldn't resist telling the wonderful news about how "her spirit came again" (Luke 8:55)—proof that she was once dead and that Jesus had brought her back to life. Jesus didn't have to touch the little girl with His hand. He could have just said a word to heal her, but it is the way of God to be tender and loving.

D. The Result (v. 26)

"And the fame of this went abroad into all that land."

You can imagine what people said about Him: "He has power over disease, He has power over disorders, and He has power over death—He can redeem. With those words Matthew reaches a pinnacle in his presentation of the power of Jesus Christ.

Conclusion

Jesus Christ is the One who holds the keys of hell and death (Rev. 1:18). For that reason, we have no need to fear death. A poet put it this way: "No longer must the mourners weep, nor call departed children dead. For death is transformed into sleep and every grave becomes a bed."

As a young man, D. L. Moody was called upon suddenly to preach a funeral sermon. He decided that he would search the gospels to find one of Christ's funeral sermons, but he searched in vain. He found that every time Christ attended a funeral, He broke it up by raising the person from the dead! And so Christ never gave a funeral sermon. When the dead heard Christ's voice, they immediately sprang to life.

We should rejoice because Christ has conquered death for us. He who would not leave His "Holy One to see corruption" (Ps. 16:10) will show us the path of life. In His presence is fullness of joy, and at His right hand are pleasures forevermore (v. 11).

I think Arthur Brisbane captured the picture of a funeral from a Christian perspective. He pictured a crowd of grieving caterpillars, all wearing black suits, mourning as they carried a cocoon to its final resting place. Above them fluttered an incredibly beautiful butterfly. Christ gives us hope, and it's a great hope, isn't it? The only thing that can sustain us is knowing that Jesus, our Savior, has power over death.

Focusing on the Facts

1. When men don't know that Christ has conquered death, what are they subject to (Heb. 2:14-15; see p. 102)?

2. Matthew 14:33, 18:26, and 20:20 each portray worship that is either hypocritical, self-serving, or true. Determine what type of worship is identified in each verse and explain why (see p. 104).

3. How did the woman of Syrophoenicia demonstrate great faith (see p. 104)?

4. What was the Father able to do through Jesus without His knowing it? Why (Luke 8:44-46; see p. 105)?

5. What are the evidences for the salvation of Bartimaeus (Mark 10:46-52), the woman who anointed Jesus' feet (Luke 7:36-50), and the leper (Luke 17:14-19; see p. 106)?

6. How did Jesus demonstrate His impartiality in healing the woman in Matthew 9:22 (see p. 107)?

7. What type of people might someone unfamiliar with God's ways expect Him to use? Instead, whom has God chosen, according to 1 Corinthians 1:26-28 (see pp. 107-8)?

8. What lesson did Peter learn in Acts 10:34 (see p. 108)?

9. Although Christians can reflect most of Jesus' attributes discussed in Matthew 9:18-26, what attribute sets Him apart from everyone else (see p. 108)?

10. When Jesus had arrived at the ruler's house, what was taking place? Why? What are some of the cultural practices that people observed at such a time (see pp. 108-9)?

11. Why did the people ridicule Jesus at the ruler's house (see p. 109)?

12. Did the people who saw Christ's miracles believe in Him? Support your answer with Scripture (see p. 110).

13. How did the parents of the girl react to Jesus' power, and what was the result (see p. 110)?

14. Why did Jesus never preach a funeral sermon (see p. 110)?

Pondering the Principles

1. Meditate upon John 5:19-29, and then answer the following questions:

   a) Can the Son act independently of the Father?

   b) According to verse 21, what can both the Father and the Son do?

   c) What authority has the Father given to the Son? Why?

   d) What is granted to the one who hears the Word of Christ and believes in the Father?

   e) When Jesus raises the dead, what two resurrection options will people face?

   If you are a believer, honoring the Father and the Son, give thanks to God that you will take part in the resurrection of life.

2. Having considering Jesus' impartiality, read James 2:1-13. Are you following Jesus' pattern of impartiality with your children, your parents, your neighbors, or your employees? Do you subconsciously give preference to those you can benefit the most from? If so, how can you begin to show equality of interest and concern to those you may have intentionally or accidentally overlooked? Praise God that he didn't look upon your wealth, your wisdom, or anything else you could offer Him when He chose you to be a child of His.

9
Miracles of Sight and Sound

Outline

Introduction
A. The Perversion of Creation
B. The Promise of God
C. The Purpose of Matthew
  1. Isaiah 29:18
  2. Isaiah 35:5-6

Lesson
  I. The Condition of the Men
 II. The Cry of the Men
   A. The Crying Described
   B. The Christ Declared
    1. The title expressed
     a) Matthew 1:1
     b) 2 Samuel 7:12-14
     c) Matthew 21:8-9
     d) Matthew 22:41-42
    2. The title evidenced
     a) Their knowledge of Messiah
     b) Their need for mercy
 III. The Confrontation with the Men
   A. The Place
   B. The Persistence
   C. The Purpose
    1. To elicit their confession
    2. To evaluate their confession
 IV. The Conversion of the Men
   A. The Manner of Healing
   B. The Measure of Faith
  V. The Command to the Men
   A. Political Problems
   B. Publicity Problems
   C. Personal Problems
 VI. The Contrariness of the Men
VII. The Commitment of the Men

Conclusion

Introduction

A. The Perversion of Creation

When God created man, He gave him dominion over the earth. Adam was king, having been given the right to rule over the created order. Man's kingdom was incredibly wondrous, for it was created by the infinite mind of God. But man sinned and lost his crown. The kingdom of light was replaced by a kingdom of darkness on this earth. Man's dominion was usurped by Satan, and because of that, there would be tears, pain, sorrow, sweat, grief, illness, injury, suffering, decay, quarreling, fighting, war, chaos, murder, lying, and ultimately, death.

B. The Promise of God

As soon as man fell, God promised that He would someday restore His kingdom to man. Someday man would again be the king of the earth. Dominion would be taken from Satan, the kingdom of darkness would end, and the kingdom of light and glory would return and last forever. Just after man has fallen in Genesis 3, God gives the promise that there will come One who will be of the seed of a woman and will bruise the serpent's (Satan's) head (v. 15). From that time on, the Old Testament is filled with promises that God will bring a Deliverer who will again establish the rule of God. That restoration would wipe out disease, death, pain, illness, sorrow, war, and fighting. The prophets repeatedly predict that this anointed Son, the King of kings, Satan's conqueror, death's defeater, sin's destroyer, and the healer of men is coming. The Jewish people knew Him as the Messiah, the Anointed One; the Prophet, Priest, and King surpassing all others. Someday, according to the Old Testament, He will come and establish His throne on the earth, making this world as God intended it to be.

C. The Purpose of Matthew

Matthew's purpose in writing is to tell us that Jesus is that Messiah and King. He will right the wrongs, reverse the curse, establish the kingdom, and destroy the enemy. And in order to convince us that Christ has the power to do that, Matthew records His miraculous power in chapters 8 and 9 as it fulfills Old Testament prophecy. Selecting only nine of Jesus' many miracles, Matthew is saying, in effect, "Jesus is the Messiah and He has given a preview of all that He will accomplish in His kingdom." That kingdom will display His power over disease, death, and disorder. In His first coming, Jesus previewed that power.

The last three miracles deal primarily with His power over death and nonfunctioning parts of the human body. That is the kind of power that will bring about the longevity of life and the resurrections that will accompany the kingdom (Isa. 65:20; Dan. 12:2). As the Messiah, Jesus demonstrated that power by raising Jairus' daughter from the dead. He showed His power over dead people and even over the dead faculties of those who were living. He healed blind eyes, dea ears, and silent tongues. Such power is prophesied in Old Testament passages.

1. Isaiah 29:18, speaking of the kingdom and the coming day when Messiah arrives, says, "And in that day shall the deaf hear the words of the book, and the eyes of the blind shall see out of obscurity, and out of darkness."

2. Isaiah 35:5-6—When the kingdom comes, "then the eyes of the blind shall be opened, and the ears of the deaf shall be unstopped. Then shall the lame man leap as an hart, and the tongue of the dumb sing."

The Old Testament said that when the Messiah came in power, the deaf would hear, the dumb would speak, the blind would see, and the lame would walk—that He would give back life to dead faculties through miracles of sight and sound. Such miracles affirmed that He was the prophesied Messiah. Matthew did not select those miracles randomly; they give us the full range of prophetic fulfillment and affirm that Jesus is none other than the promised Messiah.

As we approach the passage on miracles of sight and sound, let's set the scene. Matthew 9:27 begins, "And when Jesus departed from there." That refers to the house of Jairus in Capernaum. By that time it was evening. Jesus had a busy day raising the dead, healing the woman with an issue of blood, and perhaps engaging in dialogue with the disciples of John the Baptist and the Pharisees. As He left the house of Jairus, a mass of humanity followed Him. It was made up of the crowd that pushed their way through the narrow streets of Capernaum to the house of Jairus. They had seen Him heal the woman with the issue of blood. The crowd of mourners and musicians who witnessed the resurrection He performed followed as well. A growing crowd was returning with Jesus to the place He was staying. On the way there, Jesus performed a wonderful miracle of healing for two blind men.

Lesson

I. THE CONDITION OF THE MEN (v. 27b)

"And when Jesus departed from there, two blind men followed him."

Blindness was a common malady in Egypt, Israel, and Arabian countries. In fact, the gospel records include more healing accounts of blind people than any other type of healing, which may be an indication of its commonness. There were several causes of blindness—the unsanitary conditions that went with poverty, brilliant sunlight, excessive heat, blowing sand, accidents, war, and infectious organisms. Many people were blind from birth because of a form of gonorrhea, which was sometimes unknown even to the mother. When the baby passed through the uterus, those particular germs became lodged in the baby's eyes and began to multiply, rendering the newborn permanently blind. That is why antiseptic drops are put in the eyes of a newborn baby today, virtually eliminating that cause of blindness. That cause may have been what the disciples had in mind when they saw a blind man and asked Jesus, "Master, who did sin, this man, or his parents, that he was born blind?"

(John 9:2). They may have been wondering if he was blind as a result of that disease his parents could have contracted. There were also infective organisms that were the common cause of trachoma, a type of blindness that has been almost eliminated through the use of sulfa drugs. But before such drugs were available, blindness was a major problem.

II. THE CRY OF THE MEN (v. 27b)

"Crying, and saying, Thou Son of David, have mercy on us."

Two blind men followed Jesus, shoving their way along in their attempt to stay with the group that was leaving the neighborhood of Jairus. They boldly cried out to Jesus, having heard of Him and having possibly been part of the crowd at Jairus's house. If so, they were well aware of the resurrection that had just occurred.

What type of people follow Jesus?

It is always the broken-hearted, the bereft, the hurting, the unfit, the outcast, the discouraged, the sorrowing, the lonely, the sinful, and the guilty people who follow Jesus. You never find the self-sufficient ones who think they have all the resources or those who don't really have any questions. I once said to a certain man, "I can introduce you to Christ if you really want to know Him." But he said, "I don't want to know Him, because I don't have any need for that." The thing to do in such a situation is pray that God will bring that person to the place where he has a desperate need, because only desperate people come for help.

A. The Crying Described

The blind man and his friend were yelling or shrieking. The same Greek word is used in the gospels of insane, epileptic, or demon-possessed people who scream unintelligible words (Mark 5:5; 9:26). It is used of our Lord on the cross when He "cried out, and gave up the spirit" (Mark 15:39). It is used of a woman who was groaning with the pains of childbirth (Rev. 12:2). The word doesn't necessarily refer to intelligible speech; it can refer to cries in agony, as we see in those illustrations. The two blind men were shrieking and crying out in agony and desperation, pleading for help in the midst of their deep need. That is the desperation that often results in spiritual regeneration.

B. The Christ Declared

In addition to crying and shrieking, the blind men were intelligibly saying, "Thou Son of David, have mercy on us" (v. 27b). Why did they call Jesus of Nazareth "Son of David"? Did they know His lineage from Joseph and Mary, who were both of the line of David (Matt. 1:1; Luke 3:31)?

1. The title expressed

The title *Son of David* was the common Jewish designation for the Messiah. Matthew, aware that it would be recognized by his

Jewish readers, began his gospel with it.

a) Matthew 1:1—"The book of the genealogy of Jesus Christ, the son of David." That messianic affirmation showed that He was the Promised One. That title contained the concept of dominion and kingship of which the prophets spoke.

b) 2 Samuel 7:12-14—The promise of Messiah was given to David by God. "And when thy days be fulfilled, and thou shalt sleep with thy fathers, I will set up thy seed after thee, which shall proceed out of thine own body, and I will establish his kingdom. He shall build an house for my name, and I will establish the throne of his kingdom forever. I will be his father, and he shall be my son." Because that promise was not fully realized in Solomon, the Jewish people knew that it ultimately referred to a great Son of David who would come.

Several times Christ was recognized as the Son of David.

c) Matthew 21:8-9—As Jesus made His triumphal entry into Jerusalem, "a very great multitude spread their garments in the way; others cut down branches from the trees, and spread them in the way. And the multitudes that went before, and that followed, cried, saying, Hosanna to the Son of David! Blessed is he that cometh in the name of the Lord! Hosanna in the highest!" The crowd, acknowledging Jesus to be the Messiah, requested Him to save them with cries of "hosanna." He was coming in the Lord's name as His representative. As fickle as they were, the crowd addressed Jesus with the correct messianic title of *Son of David.*

d) Matthew 22:41-42—"While the Pharisees were gathered together, Jesus asked them, saying, What think ye of Christ? Whose son is he? They say unto him, The Son of David." In other words, everybody knew—even those who didn't believe that Jesus was the Messiah—that *the Son of David* was a title by which the Messiah was designated.

2. The title evidenced

a) Their knowledge of Messiah

When the two blind men called Jesus the "Son of David," I believe they were affirming that He was the long-awaited Messiah, the King of Israel. Perhaps they recalled Isaiah 35, which says that He would heal the blind when He came. And maybe they were aided by the far-reaching and effective ministry of John the Baptist, who heightened the anticipation of the Messiah's coming. When Jesus did the things that the Messiah was supposed to do, it became apparent to many— including the two blind men—that Jesus fulfilled their expectations, so they gave Him the messianic title.

b) Their need for mercy

The two men also cried something else that helps us know something of the genuineness of their faith. They said, "Have mercy on us." To go with their knowledge, they also had a right attitude. I believe that they felt a spiritual need as much as they felt their physical one. They believed from what they had experienced that Jesus had the power to bring the kingdom blessings. And yet they knew that they were undeserving, so they asked for mercy. That is something you never heard a Pharisee ask for, because they thought they were self-sufficient. They thought they had earned through works everything God had to give; therefore, they failed to see their need for mercy. However, the two blind men came with not only a right understanding of who Christ was, but also a right understanding of how unworthy they were. They came to the right person for mercy, because Christ was so merciful.

Let me emphasize our Lord's mercy as I quote from my book on *Kingdom Living:*

> He was the most merciful human being who ever lived. He reached out to the sick and healed them. He reached out to the crippled and gave them legs to walk. He healed the eyes of the blind, the ears of the deaf, and the mouths of the dumb. He found prostitutes and tax collectors and those who were debauched and drunken, and He drew them into the circle of His love and redeemed them and set them on their feet.

> He took the lonely and made them feel loved. He took little children and gathered them into His arms and loved them. Never was there a person on the face of the earth with the mercy of this One. Once a funeral procession came by, and He saw a mother weeping because her son was dead. She was already a widow, and now she had no child to care for her. Who would care? Jesus stopped the funeral procession, put His hand on the casket, and raised the child from the dead. He cared ([Chicago: Moody, 1980], p. 107).

Hebrews 2:17 says that our Lord was "made like his brethren, that he might be a merciful and faithful high priest." The blind men followed along, because they knew that Jesus was a merciful Messiah. They begged Him to extend mercy they knew they really didn't deserve. Apparently though, Jesus didn't acknowledge their cries; He let them continue to pour out their hearts and persistently manifest their sincerity as a way of pulling them out from the fickle, superficial crowd. If their faith was real, they would persist in following Jesus, not turning around until He healed them. In this way He tested their faith, allowing it to run to its extremity to prove its genuineness.

III. THE CONFRONTATION WITH THE MEN (v. 28)

A. The Place (v. 28a)

"And when he was come into the house."

Finally Jesus responded when He arrived at the house in which He was probably residing while in Capernaum. Possiblv Jesus lived in the house of Peter during much of His ministry in Galilee, in much the same way that He used the house of Mary, Martha, and Lazarus when He was in Judea. That was as close as He ever came to having a house of His own.

B. The Persistence (v. 28b)

"The blind men came to him."

Jesus returned home after a busy day of teaching, healing, and walking among the mass of humanity. The fact that the men even followed Jesus into the house emphasizes the utter lack of privacy that our Lord had, not to mention the relentless pressure of people who dogged His footsteps. I don't think any of us can even begin to fathom what it must have been like for Him to have those tragic people clinging to Him throughout His ministry. His moments of privacy were relatively few, unless late in the night He went away to some private place of prayer.

I see an important truth here. Every one of the healings we've seen in this chapter involves persistence, and that is how Jesus took a person past their physical healing all the way to spiritual conversion. He allowed their faith to be stretched. For example, the friends of the paralytic had to literally tear a roof apart in order to get him healed—that's persistence! They didn't say, "Hey it's crowded in there, Charlie. Let's come back another day." No. They found a way to bring their friend before Jesus. The ruler of the synagogue also showed persistence. When Jesus agreed to heal his dying daughter but stopped on the way to his house to heal the woman with an issue of blood, you can imagine how anxious the ruler was. Yet even when he found out that his daughter had died, he didn't think it was too late. He asked Jesus to bring her back to life. Even the woman who grabbed His tassel during that interlude desperately worked her way through the crowd to touch Jesus and affirmed her faith.

C. The Purpose (v. 28c)

"And Jesus saith unto them, Believe ye that I am able to do this? They said unto him, Yea, Lord."

1. To elicit their confession

Does that seem like a strange question for Jesus to ask? If it was obvious that they believed He could heal them, why did Jesus ask that question? Its purpose was not to deny their belief that He was the Messiah, nor to question whether they thought He had the power to heal. He knew they believed that. I think He asked them that to hear their own confession of faith. The apostle Paul said, "that if you confess with your mouth Jesus as Lord, and believe in your heart that God raised him from the dead, you shall be saved" (Rom. 10:9, NASB). I believe that Jesus was drawing out a verbal confession from the blind men so it would stand as a testimony to what is necessary for genuine conversion.

2. To evaluate their confession

He desired to separate them from those who were looking for a political deliverer. In effect, Jesus was asking, "Are you following Me because I am a man with charisma, or do you really believe that I represent the power of God to heal your blindness? Are you willing to affirm My lordship?" As I've said before, faith is not necessary for healing. The gospels are loaded with people whom Jesus healed; however, they didn't give evidence of having any faith. But faith is necessary for conversion, and Jesus wanted to bring those men as far as their faith would take them. When a man recognizes his need of mercy, sees that Jesus is the promised Messiah, and is willing to submit to His lordship, then he has expressed a consummate saving faith.

I believe that when the blind men said, "Yea, Lord," they were using more than just a term of respect in the sense of "sir." Because of other elements, such as their persistence, I think their use of that term was filled with all the reverence, submission, and devotion that they could offer. They made saving affirmation.

We saw the condition of the men—they were blind. We heard their cry—"Son of David, have mercy." We witnessed the confrontation—"Do you believe?" Now we come to

IV. THE CONVERSION OF THE MEN (vv. 29-30a)

"Then touched he their eyes, saying, According to your faith be it unto you. And their eyes were opened."

I believe they had more than their physical eyes opened. At that moment, the flower of faith burst into full bloom as they became children of God. Let's briefly examine both elements of healing.

A. The Manner of Healing

So often Jesus touched people to express divine tenderness in the same way that He touched the blind men's eyes. I am impressed by the simplicity of that healing. There was no fanfare. He didn't say. "Now back up, because the power's going to fly in a minute." He didn't get on a big rock and say, "Watch this." It was a simple task. because Jesus, as God, didn't need to expend a lot of energy to heal a couple of blind men. The One who can raise all who have ever died from all the graves that have ever been dug could certainly handle a couple of blind fellows. When He touched their eyes, they were opened. The men received unimaginable joy as sight burst into their conscience.

B. The Measure of Faith

What did Jesus mean by the phrase "according to your faith be it unto you"? How much faith did they have? Did they have enough faith to be healed? Yes. Did they have enough faith to be saved? Yes. If they had enough faith to be saved, then salvation is what they received. Although faith is not mandatory for healing, it is for salvation. A

120

Jesus tested their faith, He found that it was big enough to encompass redemption.

Faith in itself is nothing, as Archbishop Trench, writing on the same passage in Matthew, clearly indicates in *The Miracles of Our Lord:*

> The faith which in itself is nothing, is yet the organ for receiving everything. It is the concluding link between man's emptiness and God's fullness; and herein lies all the value it has. It is the bucket let down into the fountain of God's grace, without which the man could never draw water of life from the wells of salvation; for the wells are deep, and of himself man has nothing to draw with. It is the purse, which cannot of itself make its owner rich, and yet effectually enriches by the wealth which it contains ([London: Kegan, Paul, Trench, Trubner, 1902], p. 212).

> That's a great statement about faith, the channel through which we receive what God graciously gives us. Through their faith, the blind men received salvation from One who not only has the power to give sight, but the power to save men as well

V. THE COMMAND TO THE MEN (v. 30b)

"And Jesus strictly charged them, saying, See that no man know it."

How could the men who were blind keep everyone from knowing that they had been healed? Did this mean that they would have to go around with their eyes closed, bumping into things while pretending they were blind? The people who knew them would know otherwise. What was Jesus saying here? Jesus was very serious when He strictly charged them. The verb that Matthew used is very strong. It is also used to refer to the snorting of a horse. It conveys the idea of scolding someone in Mark 14:5. Why was Jesus so adamant about the men not telling anyone?

Some people say that Jesus wanted to hide the fact that He was a miracle worker. But it is obvious He didn't want to hide that, because He was doing miracles in public. Others simply say that He didn't want anyone to find out about the healing of the blind men. That can't be true either, because all of their friends and relatives were going to find out immediately. So there must be a different reason. I believe that He told the men not to spread the news of their healing for three reasons.

A. Political Problems

First of all, the blind men had proclaimed Jesus as the Son of David, the messianic heir to the throne of Israel, and that could have created some premature political tensions. The Jewish leaders would have immediately opposed the application of that title to Jesus, because He hadn't come up through the Jewish religious establishment. Similarly, the Romans would be threatened by the possibility of a messianic deliverer. Ultimately, it was the very affirmation that Jesus was King that brought Him to the cross. But it was not yet time for His redemptive death to take place.

B. Publicity Problems

Second, when people heard about such healings, they had a tendency to see Jesus only as a miracle worker. That kind of a conclusion resulted in dangerous and needless publicity, like that of John 6. Jesus was forced to slip away from the five thousand He had miraculously fed, because they wanted to make Him a king (v. 15). Later on, He rebuked those who continued to follow because they only wanted free food (vv. 26-27).

Jesus didn't want inaccurate publicity. It wasn't until Matthew 10 that He began to send His apostles forth with the right message. Certainly somebody as newly converted as the former blind men might present a confused message. For that reason, Jesus wanted to wait for the official ambassadors, the men He had been personally discipling, to be sent out.

C. Personal Problems

Third, I think Jesus wanted people to draw conclusions for themselves rather than make judgments about Him based on hearsay. Furthermore, if those men went beyond the circle of the people who knew them and started broadcasting what Jesus had done, people might question the reliability of their testimony. Therefore, it might be better if the people came themselves and examined the evidence before they made such conclusions.

Jesus didn't want a fickle movement to enthrone Him as a king. Neither did He want to be followed by a lot of unrepentant people who didn't understand the nature of His kingdom and were merely looking for a circus atmosphere. He didn't want others to start a revolutionary uprising on His behalf. So Jesus warned them about not saying anything.

VI. THE CONTRARINESS OF THE MEN (v. 31)

"But they, when they were departed, spread abroad his fame in all that country."

The men did exactly what Jesus told them not to do. However, that is understandable. If you had been blind and were given sight, you would probably tell others about it with a lot excitement. Usually we have the opposite problem. The Lord wants us to say things, but we don't. However, there are times when He doesn't want us to say things, but we do. In that case, I guess it was a sin only a grateful heart could commit, but it was nonetheless a sin. They were commanded not to speak, but they disobeyed the command. Fortunately, the story doesn't end there.

VII. THE COMMITMENT OF THE MEN (vv. 32-33a)

"As they went out, behold, they brought to him a dumb man [Gk., *kōphos,* "one deaf or dumb"; cf. Matt. 11:5)] possessed with a demon. And when the demon was cast out, the dumb spoke."

We might doubt whether they were genuinely children of God if all they did was disobey immediately. So Matthew records the evidence of their salvation. The two who had been blind immediately got hold of a friend and brought him to Jesus. This fellow beggar was deaf, a very common disability caused by infections within the ear, congenital defects, and blowing sand. But he was deaf and mute as a result of being possessed by a demon. It is possible for demons to affect people in a physical way, as Scripture clearly indicates. But when the Lord, who has power over the kingdom of darkness, cast the demon out, "the dumb spoke" (v. 33a). The verse doesn't even tell us how the Lord did it. Matthew doesn't make a big fanfare about His power here because there was so much of it, and casting out a demon was a simple thing for Him. Again, may I draw your attention to the fact that the passage says nothing about the man's faith. We don't know if he even knew what was going on when he was healed. We do know, however, that the blind men had faith enough to be saved and to immediately become useful to Christ in bringing others to Him. I'm glad the story ends that way. They were weak and disobedient, but they also were committed enough to bring a fellow beggar to Christ.

Conclusion

I think this simple story contains one of the most beautiful analogies of salvation in all of Matthew's gospel. The men's blindness is an analogy of the spiritual blindness that is caused by sin. The story provides an outline for the logical (although not necessarily chronological) sequence in salvation.

A. A Need

First of all, the two blind men had a need. They were blind. That's where salvation begins—nobody comes to God unless he senses a need and knows that he cannot see. A person must recognize that he has no resources, no hope, and that he cannot discern the truth.

B. Knowledge

They found out that Jesus was the Messiah, the Son of David. Their knowledge was right. Out of their need came their knowledge—they sought to know the truth, and they found it.

C. A Sense of Sinfulness

They said, "Have mercy on us. We're not here to tell You that we deserve anything; we're here to tell You that we need something." When you need salvation, you come with a cry for mercy.

D. Faith

They persistently followed the Lord, crying out to Him as evidence of their faith. The Old Testament says, "And ye shall seek me, and find me, when ye shall search for me with all your heart" (Jer. 29:13).

E. Confession

When asked if they believed in Christ's ability to heal them, the two blind men said, "Yes Lord." That was an affirmation of their submission and devotion to the lordship of Christ.

F. Conversion

Their conversion is implied in the phrase "according to your faith be it unto you" (v. 29). And do you know what often follows conversion?

G. Weakness

Disobedience can occur when you are a newborn babe in Christ. You don't know how to discern between right and wrong and can therefore be "tossed to and fro, and carried about with every wind of doctrine" (Eph. 4:14). Spiritual babes who are weak in knowing and applying biblical truths are susceptible to disobedience, in spite of their zeal.

H. Usefulness

Intermingled with their disobedience was their desire to bring somebody else to Jesus Christ. That is often true of new Christians. They just grab the nearest person and introduce him to the Lord. I believe that the Lord healed the man they brought to Him in order to show those two blind men that they were going to be useful to Him in the advancement of His kingdom.

Jesus is the Messiah. If you haven't yet come to that conclusion, you are living in opposition to all the evidence. If you've not experienced the conversion that we have seen in the lives of these men, you are yet in the darkness of your sin. That is needless, for Christ offers Himself as the One who dispels the darkness. Let me close with some appropriate words of George Lansing Taylor:

> O Saviour, we are blind and dumb,
> To Thee for sight and speech we come;
> Touch Thou our eyes with truth's bright rays,
> Teach Thou our lips to sing Thy praise.

> Help us to feel our mournful night,
> And seek, through all things, for Thy light,
> Till the glad sentence we receive,
> "Be it to you as you believe."

> Then swift the dumb to Thee we'll bring,
> Till all Thy grace shall see, and sing.

Focusing on the Facts

1. What types of healing did the Old Testament prophesy the Messiah would accomplish when He came (Isa. 35:5-6; see pp. 114-15)?

2. Why was blindness a major problem in Jesus' time (see p. 115)?

3. What type of people follow Jesus (see p. 116)?

4. What can we do for a person who hasn't recognized his or her need for Christ (see p. 116)?

5. Describe the crying of the blind men (see p. 116).

6. How did the blind men address Jesus? What was meant by such a title (see pp. 116-17)?

7. What did the blind men request from Jesus? Why (see pp. 117-18)?

8. Why would we probably never read of a Pharisee asking for mercy (see p. 118)?

9. Cite some examples of ways Jesus showed mercy to others (see p. 118).

10. Why might Jesus have let the blind men follow Him without immediately answering their cries (see p. 118)?

11. Where might Jesus have stayed while living in Capernaum of Galilee? Where might He have stayed in Judea (see pp. 118-19)?

12. What was Jesus doing by asking the blind men if they thought He could heal them (see p. 119)?

13. What can we learn about Jesus from His manner of healing the blind men (see p. 120)?

14. Explain Trench's two analogies of faith (see p. 121).

15. What could be two of the reasons that Jesus commanded the men to not spread around the news of the their healing (see pp. 121-22)?

16. Rather than follow Jesus' instruction, what did the two men do? Why (see p. 122)?

17. How did the men demonstrate their commitment to Jesus (see p. 122)?

18. What does the account of the blind men serve as an analogy of (see p. 123)?

19. Why is it that those who have become Christians can so easily disobey (see p. 124)?

Pondering the Principles

1. The two blind men came to Jesus with the right attitude and the right acknowledgment. They humbly sought mercy, and they recognized Christ as the Messiah. How are those two elements applicable to salvation (John 5:39-40; 8:24)? In what way does everyone need mercy (Rom. 3:23)? Make a list of five people you personally know who are not believers. What do you think that each of them lacks—the right attitude, the right acknowledgment, or both? Knowing what they need, determine to study the Bible and share things with them that can lead them to salvation.

2. Privacy is an element that our society cherishes. Unfortunately, our privacy can turn us into isolationists if we're not careful. Do you recall the general pattern of Jesus' availability to people with little concern for His own privacy? Does your life-style have the proper balance of privacy and availability to those believers and unbelievers who can benefit from your witness? Do you take time to rest physically and spiritually refresh yourself in communion with God? Do you also sacrificially give of your time and privacy so that you may make an impact on others for the glory of Christ?

3. If God were to grade your faith in Him at this moment, would you receive an A, B, C, D, or F? Do you feel like your spiritual life is stagnant, or do you have great expectations for the things that God can do through you? If your faith seems weak, maybe you need to exercise it on a regular basis by trusting that God can use you beyond what you ever thought possible. Have you made yourself available to God like the prophet Isaiah, who said, "Here I am; send me" (Isa. 6:8b)? The more you trust God, the more you will receive of His fullness and be useful to Him (see p. 124).

10
Responding to Jesus' Power

Outline

Introduction
A. The Dividing Line Prophesied
  1. Luke 2
  2. Luke 1
B. The Dividing Line Proclaimed
  1. Luke 6
  2. Matthew 7
  3. Matthew 10
  4. Matthew 21
  5. 2 Corinthians 2

Lesson
I. The Works of the Lord
  A. "Teaching in Their Synagogues"
    1. The place of teaching
      a) The history of synagogues
      b) The service of synagogues
      c) The functions of synagogues
        (1) A court of law
        (2) A theological school
        (3) A place for the exposition of Scripture
    2. The pattern of teaching
      a) Reading the passage
      b) Teaching the passage
      c) Responding to the passage
  B. "Preaching the Gospel of the Kingdom"
  C. "Healing Every Sickness and Every Disease"
II. The Response of the People
  A. The Marveling Multitude
    1. The meaning of their marveling
    2. The fickleness of their following
  B. The Rejecting Religionists

Conclusion

Introduction

In our last chapter, we stopped at verse 33 with the healing of a man who was deaf and dumb because of a demon. Matthew immediately follows that miracle with a statement of response, "And the multitudes marveled, saying, It was never so seen in Israel. But the Pharisees said, He casteth out demons through the prince of the demons. And Jesus went about all the cities and villages, teaching in their synagogues, and preaching the gospel of the kingdom, and healing every sickness and every disease among the people" (33*b*-35). Matthew gives us two responses to the miracles that Jesus had done. There was the marveling of the multitude and the rejection of the religionists.

A. The Dividing Line Prophesied

   1. Luke 2

   When our Lord was a baby, probably no more than forty days old, He was taken by His mother and Joseph to the Temple in Jerusalem. The law required that she make an offering of purification after giving birth to a child. While they were in the Temple, they had occasion to meet a very interesting man by the name of Simeon. He had been waiting a long time for the arrival of the Messiah and now had the privilege of seeing Him. When he saw Jesus, he said that "mine eyes have seen thy salvation. . . . And Simeon blessed them, and said unto Mary, his mother, Behold, this child is set for the fall and rising again of many in Israel" (vv. 30, 34). Simeon stated that Jesus would become the dividing line. He would determine the ultimate destiny of every individual. Some will reject Him and fall; some will receive Him and rise again.

   It's always been that way in God's economy. There are those who are planted like a tree by a river and bring forth fruit, and there are those who are chaff (Ps. 1). There are the godly and the ungodly, the righteous and the unrighteous. My grandfather used to say, "The only two kinds of people in the world are the saints and the ain'ts."

   2. Luke 1

   Even Mary, in general terms, spoke of God's judicial role of separating the faithful and the unfaithful. She praised God after learning of the greatness of the child she would bear, "And his mercy is on them that fear him from generation to generation. He hath shown strength with his arm; he hath scattered the proud in the imagination of their hearts. He hath put down the mighty from their seats, and exalted them of low degree. He hath filled the hungry with good things; and the rich he hath sent empty away" (vv. 50-53). Mary knew that it was characteristic of God to receive some and refuse others, to bless some and curse others, to gather some in and scatter others, to pull down the exalted and lift up the humble, to fill the hungry and send away the full. In other words, there will always be the dividing line between those God blesses and those He curses. Mary knew that because she knew the Old Testament. It was confirmed to her by Simeon that her child would be the very crux of destiny.

B. The Dividing Line Proclaimed

1. Luke 6

Christ Himself affirmed that when He taught: "And he lifted up his eyes on his disciples, and said, Blessed be ye poor; for yours is the kingdom of God. Blessed are ye that hunger now; for ye shall be filled. Blessed are ye that weep now; for ye shall laugh. Blessed are ye, when men shall hate you, and when they shall separate you from their company, and shall reproach you, and cast out your name as evil, for the Son of man's sake. Rejoice ye in that day, and leap for joy; for, behold, your reward is great in heaven; for in the like manner did their fathers unto the prophets. But woe unto you that are rich! For ye have received your consolation. Woe unto you that are full! For ye shall hunger. Woe unto you that laugh now! For ye shall mourn and weep. Woe unto you, when all men shall speak well of you! For so did their fathers to the false prophets" (vv. 20-26). There are the blessed, and there are the cursed.

2. Matthew 7

There are those who enter the narrow gate and are blessed, and those who enter the broad gate and are damned (vv. 13-14). There are those who build their house upon a rock that stands in judgment, and there are those who build their house on sand that collapses (vv. 24-27).

3. Matthew 10

There are those who try to hold onto their lives and lose them, and there are those who lose their lives, and in so doing, find them (v. 39). All the way through the gospel, which records for us the thrust of the preaching of Jesus, we find that He offers Himself as a dividing line. He told those who would be His disciples, "Whosoever, therefore, shall confess me before men, him will I confess also before my Father, who is in heaven" (v. 32). In other words, if you identify yourself with Jesus Christ, God will identify you as His own. But if you deny Jesus Christ, then Christ will deny you before the Father. Jesus went on to say, "Think not that I am come to send peace on earth; I came not to send peace, but a sword. For I am come to set a man at variance against his father, and the daughter against her mother, and the daughter-in-law against her mother-in-law. And a man's foes shall be they of his own household" (vv. 34-36).

4. Matthew 21

Confronting the hypocrisy of the chief priests and the elders, Jesus spoke in a parable, "But what think ye? A certain man had two sons; and he came to the first, and said, Son, go work today in my vineyard. He answered and said, I will not; but afterward he repented, and went. And he came to the second, and said the same. And he answered and said, I go, sir; and went not. Which of the two did the will of his father? They say unto him, The first. Jesus saith unto them, Verily I say unto you that the tax collectors and the harlots go into the kingdom of God before you" (vv. 28-31). In other words, the first son was disobedient to his father, but later repented and obeyed. The second son pretended to be submissive, but he didn't go. The son who said no and repented represented the tax collectors and the harlots. The son who said he would go but didn't symbolized the hypocritical religionists. Jesus again presented the dividing line. It isn't the ones who are religious who will enter heaven; it is the ones who obey the will of God. The Father expressed His will when He spoke from heaven and said, "This is my beloved Son, in whom I am well pleased; hear ye him" (Matt. 17:5*b*). Christ is the demarcation line for all people.

5. 2 Corinthians 2

The apostle Paul continued that same concept. The entire human race is divided into believers and unbelievers, into heaven-bound and hell-bound souls, into the blessed and the cursed, and into the rewarded and the damned. The dividing line is their faith or lack of faith in the Lord Jesus Christ. "Now thanks be unto God, who always causeth us to triumph in Christ, and maketh manifest the savor of his knowledge by us in every place" (v. 14). In other words, there's a certain fragrance that a Christian has, a certain exuding representation of God. We touch the world, as it were, with the fragrance of God. "For we are unto God a sweet savor of Christ, in them that are saved, and in them that perish: to the one we are the savor of death unto death; and to the other, the savor of life unto life" (vv. 15-16*a*).

Paul is saying that Christians, as they preach the gospel, are actually radiating that reality to the saved and the perishing. To the perishing, the message is a fragrance of death unto death. Already dead in their rejection, the more they hear the gospel, the deeper their lostness becomes. The perishing constantly tread under their feet the Son of God and count the blood of the covenant an unholy thing (Heb. 10:29). That results in an increased deadness. They are compounding their doom, which becomes all the more terrible as they continue to reject the truth. On the other hand, as we preach the gospel to those who are already alive in Christ, we give off a savor of life unto life—an enriched understanding of the fullness of life in Christ.

Jesus is the dividing line, and Matthew makes that abundantly clear in chapters 8 and 9. Matthew wants us to understand that because Christ is the Messiah, a decision must be made. A British school supervisor wrote that the problem with the age we are living in is that we are standing at the crossroads, and the signposts have fallen down. But not according to Matthew, because he points them out very clearly and calls us to make the right choice by believing in Christ. In order to help us, he presents irrefutable evidence that Christ is the Son of God, the Messiah, and the Savior. He shows us the narrow way, the way of faith in Christ. To convince us that Christ is who He claims to be, Matthew records nine miracles in chapters 8 and 9 that are beyond the capacity of any human being—not only to perform but even to fathom. They are not the full scope of all of His miracles, but are only samples, as John indicates in his gospel: "And many other signs truly did Jesus in the presence of his disciples, which are not written in this book" (20:30). He also said that if His miracles "should be written every one, I suppose that even the world itself could not contain the books that should be written" (21:25).

Lesson

I. THE WORKS OF THE LORD (v. 35)

The verb in the phrase "and Jesus went about" has the idea of a constant, incessant effort. Such an effort would be necessary in order to visit "all the cities and villages" of Gaililee, as 4:23 indicates. That area is in the northern part of the country and is relatively fertile. Much of the food was grown there. Josephus tells us that at the time of Jesus there were probably 204 towns and villages. The difference between a city and a village was the existence of a wall around a city. Little villages didn't fortify themselves, but cities did. Galilee was about seventy miles long by forty miles wide. Josephus writes, "The cities are numerous and the multitude of villages everywhere crowded with men, owing to the fertility of the soil, so that the smallest of them contains above 1500 inhabitants." He estimated that there were three million people in just the area of Galilee. For Jesus to have reached them all, He must have moved rapidly through all the villages and towns—healing, preaching, and teaching. Those three ministries would each require a great deal of time to study if taken by themselves, so we will get a brief overview of them.

A. "Teaching in Their Synagogues"

  1. The place of teaching

    a) The history of synagogues

      Wherever there were Jewish people, there was a synagogue This gathering place was the center of Jewish community life It was the focal point of religious belief, the town hall, and the local court, among other things. The synagogue was a late addition to Judaism, not appearing until the Babylonian captivity Before that time, the worship of the faithful had been focused on the Temple. But when the Temple was destroyed and the Jewish people were taken out of their country into Babylon for seventy years, they began to assemble together in synagogues That practice continues to this day because the Temple has never been rebuilt since its last destruction. Even today synagogues exist in every city of the world in which there are Jewish people.

In the time of our Lord, there were synagogues in all the little towns and villages in Palestine. They were usually built on a hill or the highest spot in the area. If there weren't any high spots, they were built by a river. Very often, their tops were left open—as the Temple's had been—so the people could see God's creation and look up to heaven as part of their worship. The synagogue normally was identified by a tall pole that shot right up into the air, much like the steeple on a New England church marks each little town. Consequently, any Jewish person who was a stranger in town could just follow his way to the pole to find the synagogue.

b) The service of synagogues

Every Sabbath, the people would meet together for worship. Services were also held on the second and fifth days of every week, as well as on every festival day. The service was very simple, not unlike the service of the church today. It began with thanksgivings, or "blessings" as they were called, much like a church might begin by singing praises. The people would speak of blessing of the Lord and express thankfulness for what He had done. That was followed by a prayer that was concluded by a responding amen from the congregation. Then a prescribed reader would stand up and read from the law of Moses in the Hebrew, the original language of its writing. He would translate it into Aramaic, the common language of the day. Next would come a reading of a passage from one of the prophets, which also would be translated. Then there would be a sermon, or an exhortation. The service would close with a benediction and a final amen from the people.

c) The functions of synagogues

The Jewish people always thought of the synagogue as a place of teaching. In fact, the Yiddish word for synagogue is *schul,* much like our word *school.* But the synagogue served a variety of purposes.

(1) A court of law

The Jewish people resided in occupied countries. They were often granted self-governing jurisdiction by the occupying government. Such authority was exercised in their synagogues. For example, our Lord warned His disciples that the Jewish leaders would scourge them in their synagogues (Matt. 10:17). They would render the verdict and even carry out the punishment in the synagogue.

(2) A theological school

The synagogue was used for training boys in the Talmud and was, in a sense, a theological school. The affairs of the synagogue were administered by ten of the elders, three of which were identified as rulers. They also acted as judges.

A fourth elder was called the messenger of the assembly and served as the leader. One was the interpreter who translated the Hebrew into Aramaic, and another ran the theological school. In other words, they had divisions of responsibility as elders.

(3) A place for the exposition of Scripture

Philo said that synagogues were mainly for the detailed reading and exposition of Scripture. We find the same emphasis on the teaching of Scripture in Acts 17. The apostle Paul found his way to the little town of Berea and "went into the synagogue of the Jews" (v. 10). When he preached to them, "they received the word with all readiness of mind, and searched the scriptures daily, whether those things were so" (v. 11).

When the sermon was presented on any given day, it could be preached by any leading member of the congregation who was erudite or knowledgeable in Scripture. If there happened to be a visiting dignitary or rabbi, it was customary to let that rabbi preach the sermon. That custom seems almost divinely designed, for it perfectly suited the needs of our Lord and His itinerant preachers as they presented the gospel within the Jewish culture. Jesus, Paul, and others always had access to preaching and teaching in synagogues.

2. The pattern of teaching

The mode of teaching in a synagogue was the exposition of Scripture. They read it, explained it, and applied it. In Nehemiah, the Levites "read in the book in the law of God distinctly, and gave the sense, and caused them to understand the reading" (8:8). Sometimes people have asked me why I teach the Bible the way I do, saying it is different from what their church does. But the exposition of Scripture is not anything new. That method has early beginnings and should still be used.

a) Reading the passage

Luke also tells us that Jesus taught in the synagogues (4:15) providing a good illustration of how He did it: "And he came to Nazareth, where he had been brought up; and, as his custom was, he went into the synagogue on the sabbath day, and stood up to read. And there was delivered unto him the book of the prophet, Isaiah. And when he had opened the book, he found the place where it was written, The Spirit of the Lord is upon me, because he hath anointed me to preach the gospel to the poor; he hath sent me to heal the brokenhearted, to preach deliverance to the captives, and recovering of sight to the blind, to set at liberty them that are bruised, to preach the acceptable year of the Lord" (4:16-19). Every person in the synagogue knew that passage referred to the Messiah.

132

b) Teaching the passage

"And he closed the book, and he gave it again to the minister, and sat down [the normal position for teaching]. And the eyes of all them that were in the synagogue were fastened on him. And he began to say unto them, This day is this scripture fulfilled in your ears" (vv. 20-21). In effect, Jesus said, "I am the living fulfillment of that passage. I am the proper interpretation of that text." That was fairly shocking news for them. And after He had said some other shocking remarks, the people in the synagogue were stimulated to respond.

c) Responding to the passage

"And all they in the synagogue, when they heard these things, were filled with wrath, and rose up, and thrust him out of the city, and led him unto the brow of the hill on which their city was built, that they might cast him down headlong. But he, passing through the midst of them, went his way" (vv. 28-30).

So Jesus taught in the synagogues by expositing the Word of God. In His case, He was the very application of His teaching. But the people didn't like His interpretation at all and tried to kill Him. He went through all the villages and cities teaching in the synagogues, although He probably didn't always have to escape for His life. The reason I believe in expository preaching is that it was the method Jesus used. And I believe that preaching style should still be emphasized when God's people gather together.

B. "Preaching the Gospel of the Kingdom"

What does it mean to say He was preaching? The Greek word is *kērussō* and means "to herald, to make a public announcement or proclamation." Jesus didn't limit Himself to teaching expositorily in the synagogues; He was also out on the street corners, on the hillsides, by the sea, in the houses, along the roadway, and in the fields preaching the gospel of the kingdom. It was geared more toward evangelism than teaching and was often directed to those who were outside the religious environment. His message was always the same—good news (which is what *gospel* means). The good news is that the kingdom, which the Jewish people had waited so long for, had finally arrived. That was not an exposition of the Old Testament like He was giving in the synagogue. Such preaching was the proclamation of the New Covenant—the unfolding of the mysteries that had been hidden from people in the past. Mention of the kingdom came up often in His preaching. "Blessed are the poor in spirit; for theirs is the kingdom of heaven" (Matt. 5:3). "But seek ye first the kingdom of God" (Matt. 6:33). "After this manner, therefore, pray ye. . . . Thy kingdom come" (Matt. 6:9-10).

That kingdom was not just a future one. When He was preaching about the kingdom, He was calling people to believe in Him. The moment anyone did so, he entered the kingdom. In the words of Paul, a believer is delivered from the power of darkness, for God has "translated us into the kingdom of his dear Son" (Col. 1:13). Being born again is an instantaneous transaction. You are in the kingdom if you're a Christian. Christ is the King who rules the lives of His subjects. He feeds us with the resources of His unlimited riches. So the kingdom can be entered now through the narrow gate that He spoke of in Matthew 7. He offered entrance into the kingdom to all who would believe in Him and receive the numerous blessings that accompanied it.

Jesus' exposition of the Old Testament and proclamation of the New Covenant highlight the importance of having both of those ministries in the church today. We must come together for the exposition of the Word of God, and we must go out into the highways and byways to proclaim the gospel of the kingdom.

C. "Healing Every Sickness and Every Disease"

In importance, the use of miracles was third, because it was not the main issue. Jesus' ministry involving miracles merely affirmed the validity of the ministries previously mentioned. B. B. Warfield in *Counterfeit Miracles* said, "When our Lord came down to earth, He drew heaven with Him. The signs that accompanied His ministry were but the trailing clouds of glory that He brought from heaven, which is His home." Miracles proved that the kingdom was at hand, because they were samples of what the Messiah would do when the kingdom came. There was no way to refute them. In fact, the Pharisees never denied His miracles; they only denied the source of them. They were literally overwhelming.

II. THE RESPONSE OF THE PEOPLE (vv. 33b-34)

It doesn't take very long to see what that was. We've already seen some responses. The first three miracles that Matthew recorded in chapter 8 had a response. Three men said they wanted to follow the Lord, but they loved personal comfort, personal riches, and personal relationships more than Christ, so they turned their backs on Him and walked away. They illustrate a superficial interest that never comes to fruition. It is a momentary response of fascination that has no true root to it.

Following the second set of miracles came the responses of Matthew's conversion, the irritation of the Pharisees, and the confusion of the disciples of John the Baptist. There are people like Matthew who really believe in Christ and bring all their friends to Him; there are people like the Pharisees who get irritated at what Jesus says because He confronts the status quo; and there are also people like followers of John the Baptist, who all their lives had been in one religious system and now were confused about the new things that they were hearing.

Now we come to the third set of responses. The multitude marveled at Christ's works, and the religionists rejected them, saying that Jesus did them by the power of Satan. They couldn't deny that He did them; they just denied that their source was God. In Matthew's selection of miracles in chapter 9, he picked out some wonderful miracles. People not only were healed but were also redeemed: the paralytic (v. 2), the publican—Matthew himself (v. 9), the ruler (v. 18), the woman with the issue of blood (vv. 20-21), the blind men (v. 28). So we've seen some with a right response who have really believed along the way. But there will also be those who are fickle, those who are irritated, and those who are confused. In that light, Matthew is calling all of us to make the right decision.

A. The Marveling Multitude (v. 33*b*)

"And the multitudes marveled, saying, It was never so seen in Israel."

The multitude concluded that the miracles they had seen were, without question, the greatest display of power ever witnessed by anybody in the history of Israel. They would have remembered Moses, Elijah, and Elisha and the miracles of their times. They could talk about the drowning of the Egyptian Army, the writing of the law in stone at Mount Sinai, the fall of Jericho, and so on. They had heard about wondrous things in the past, but never had anything been seen like Christ's miracles. They were a display of divine power that was unequaled in Jewish history. Is it any wonder they marveled?

1. The meaning of their marveling

The word *marvel* (Gk., *thaumazō*) is a very comprehensive word. It means that they were amazed or astonished. When accompanied by a prefix (Gk., *ekthaumazō*), the word means "to marvel greatly" as in Mark 12:17. When used with the particle *lian*, it means "to marvel exceedingly." They were amazed beyond amazement at what He did. It was breathtaking and incomprehensible to their human minds to see the things He was doing. They were in awe. The word also includes the idea of terror or fear, as in the case of the disciples who were more afraid when Jesus stopped the storm than they were when the storm was threatening to take their life (Matt. 8:23-27). They knew they were in a boat with God. When you know that He can see everything in your heart, that has to be terrorizing!

2. The fickleness of their following

Luke 9:43 sums up why Jesus astounded the multitudes: "And they were all astonished at the mighty power of God. But while they marveled every one at all things which Jesus did." The people were so fascinated with what Jesus was doing that they could make only one conlcusion, "And the multitudes that went before, and that followed, cried, saying, Hosanna to the Son of David! Blessed is he that cometh in the name of the Lord! Hosanna in the highest!" (Matt. 21:9). The marveling multitude that threw palm branches at the feet of the One they acknowledged to be the Messiah is the same multitude that turned against Him when they got word that He was preaching a message that the establishment didn't want to hear. The same crowd that praised Jesus in Matthew 21 turned around in Matthew 27 and screamed for Him to be

135

crucified and Barabbas to be released (vv. 20-25). But that's how it is with fickle mobs with a superficial fascination. They are like those in John 6 who followed Christ for free food—they really weren't interested in what He had to say. They liked Him at a distance; they were fascinated enough to follow, but afraid of close contact.

Fickle Fascination

I'm amazed at how people today are eager to see movies that scare them to death, even if it means that they have to run out into the lobby during the scary scenes. Why would people line up for blocks to see such movies as *The Exorcist*? There's a certain fascination, I guess, as long as you're sitting in a soft seat, shoving popcorn into your mouth, and you can leave when it's over. People don't want to actually experience terror, but it's all right to watch somebody else in it.

In a similar way, I believe there was something of that fascination in people who were terrified of Christ but were also astounded and amazed at the supernatural. Like those who watch horror movies, they wanted to make sure Jesus remained at an arm's length. When He challenged the status quo, their fascination ended, and they wanted Him dead.

Many people, including those following, have been in awe of Jesus, but didn't know Him as their Lord, as far as we know. Consequently, they will spend eternity in hell in spite of the favorable things that they said about Jesus.

Pontius Pilate said He was a man without fault.

Diderot (the French philosopher) said He was the unsurpassed.

Napoleon (the French emperor) said He was the emperor of love.

Strauss (the German theologian and philosopher) said He was the highest model of religion.

John Stuart Mill (the English philosopher and economist) said He was the guide of humanity.

Lecky (the Irish historian and essayist) said He was the highest pattern of virtue.

Martineau (the English theologian and philosopher) said He was the divine flower of humanity.

Renan (the French philologist and historian) said He was the greatest among the sons of men.

Theodore Parker (an American Unitarian clergyman) said He was the youth with God in His heart.

Robert Owen (the Welsh social reformer) said He was the irreproachable.

And Broadway said He was a superstar. People have always thrown kind epithets at Him. In His own day, many said, "What manner of man is this?" (Matt. 8:27). They didn't have a category for Him

Even in contemporary Christianity there is a fascination with Jesus. People applaud Him. They like Him as long as He's sort of warm and fuzzy, without being confrontive. As long as He is identified with love and sweetness and kept at arm's length, He is a fascinating personality. You can talk about Jesus all you want if you don't confront people with the fact that He condemns men who commit immorality; who cheat or lie; who are homosexuals, adulterers, or fornicators; or who fail to live by God's law. When the fickle find out that Jesus sends those kinds of people to an eternal hell, they're not so thrilled about it all. As a case in point, I was told by a pastor about some Christian students who were holding a meeting at California State University, Long Beach, to affirm the biblical standards of morality. They had been received fairly well until, at one session on homosexuality, a homosexual faculty member marched down the aisle screaming profanity while the speaker was talking. Afterwards, some of the gay community at that school were spitting on the Christian students. Jesus is OK as long as you don't confront sin.

As soon as the multitude got close enough to find out what Jesus was really saying, their tune changed fast. They discovered that it was not safe to deal with a holy person—except at an arm's length. Such an attitude was typical of the Pharisees, who were always honoring the prophets, but were no better than their forefathers who killed them (Matt. 23:29-35). The only prophet that was alive in Jesus' time was John the Baptist, and Herodias had him killed. Similarly, when Jesus became a threat to the religious leaders, they had Him killed. The crowd kept their distance in a strange fascination, but when they got too close to Him toward the end of Jesus' ministry, they joined

B. The Rejecting Religionists (v. 34)

"But the Pharisees said, He casteth out demons through the prince of the demons."

They saw that He had cast a demon out of a man who couldn't hear or speak. They couldn't deny that He had done that; however, they attributed His power to the prince of demons. Jesus showed how illogical their conclusion was when He said to them if Satan cast out his own demons, he would be defeating his own purpose (Matt. 12:25-27). Because of their refusal to believe the truth, the Pharisees committed themselves to eliminating Jesus. It is no wonder that Jesus said if they didn't believe Moses and the prophets, they wouldn't believe even if somebody miraculously came back from the dead (Luke 16:31). They had sunk to such a tragic depth that they made the very opposite conclusion of the one the miracles were designed to produce.

Both of those kinds of responses are wrong—both will cause those who hold them to end up in hell forever, whether they belong to the hating rejectors who blasphemed and said Jesus was of Satan, or to the multitude that marveled and followed Him in mere fascination. The proper response is to believe and receive Christ, not merely to be fascinated by Him—that's inadequate for salvation.

Conclusion

So Matthew has given us a good picture of possible responses to Christ. There are people who say, "I want to be Your disciple. I'm going to follow You, but I've got personal comforts, riches, and relationships now, so I don't think I'd better come yet." Then there are those like Matthew, who come immediately and bring friends who are burdened with their sins. There are also angry religionists who start out being irritated, become blasphemers, and ultimately end up as murderers. There are confused people, like the disciples of John the Baptist, who just can't figure out why Jesus did what He did (Matt. 9:14-15). Maybe they've been raised in a different religion, and they're trying to make sense out of Christianity. Finally, there's a great mass of humanity that doesn't fit into any of those categories. They are what I call "the marveling multitude." They say, "Jesus is so nice. Christmas and Easter are wonderful. I listen to Jesus pop music all the time." Those superficial followers are content to stand at arm's length and watch Jesus do His thing. But ultimately, they stand with crucifiers screaming for His blood. So mark carefully, beloved, where you make your choice, for Jesus is set for the rise and fall of many.

Focusing on the Facts

1. When Jesus was brought into the Temple as a baby, what did Simeon declare that Jesus would become (Luke 2:34; see p. 127)?

2. From a biblical perspective, what are the only two types of people in the world (see p. 127)?

3. Although someone has written that we are standing at the crossroads where the signposts have fallen down, Matthew put them up again. How did he do that (see pp. 129-30)?

4. Give a brief history of the synagogue (pp. 130-31).

5. What were some of the functions of the synagogue (see pp. 131-32)?

6. Primarily, what were the synagogues used for (see p. 132)?

7. Who would normally preach in the synagogues? Who else would be allowed to preach? How does that custom seem divinely designed (see p. 132)?

8. Identify and explain the mode of teaching in Nehemiah 8:8 (see p. 132)

9. How did Jesus interpret the reading of Isaiah in Luke 4:15-21 (see p. 133)?

10. How did Jesus' preaching differ from His teaching with regard to place audience, and content (see p. 133)?

11. In what sense is the kingdom that Jesus was preaching about a presen reality (see p. 134)?

12. In importance, where do the miracles of Christ stand in relation to Hi teaching and preaching? Why (see p. 134)?

13. Although the Pharisees couldn't deny that Jesus had done miracles, wha did they deny (see p. 137)?

14. What did the multitudes conclude about the miracles they had seen (see p. 135)?

15. What was the crowd's response when Jesus entered Jerusalem in Matthew 21:9? How did they respond a week later in Matthew 27:20-25 (see pp. 135-36)?

16. Why did the crowd follow Jesus? Why did they, for the most part, avoid close contact (see p. 136)?

17. In spite of the favorable things that many people have said about Jesus, why will some of them spend eternity in hell (see pp. 136-37)?

18. Many people think of Jesus as a fascinating personality. But what don't they want to hear (see pp. 136-37)?

19. Who did the Pharisees attribute Jesus' power to? Why was this illogical, according to Jesus (see p. 137)?

Pondering the Principles

1. Read through the parable from Matthew 21:28-31 on pages 128-29. Which son most closely represents your life? Do you find yourself initially resisting but ultimately obeying, or outwardly agreeing while inwardly refusing to obey? Which response is clearly more pleasing to God, according to the parable? Are you currently living out God's will on a regular basis? Read James 1:21-27. How are you proving yourself to be a doer of the Word? Make a personal commitment to apply the Scripture you receive. Find someone that will hold you accountable to be "an effectual doer" (v. 25, NASB).

2. Sometimes we think that the destiny of those we share Christ with lies solely in our hands. Keep in mind that Christ said, "Think not that I am come to send peace on earth; I came not to send peace, but a sword" (Matt. 10:34). Can knowing that He—not us—is the dividing line of people's destiny make our jobs as ambassadors any easier? Why? Are you intimidated to share your faith with others because you fear being personally rejected? Consider yourself to be a tourist who has found the right road and is merely pointing out the signs that show the way to eternal life.

3. If you are truly committed to Christ, then you must realize that you cannot necessarily expect to be a popular person—in spite of what Christianity in the media may lead you to believe. Jesus told the first leaders of Christianity (His disciples) that the world would hate them (John 15:18-19) and even try to kill them, thinking they were doing God a favor (John 16:1-2). Paul told the Corinthians that serving Christ meant that one had to be willing to make sacrifices and suffer persecution (1 Cor. 4:11-13; 2 Tim. 3:12). When was the last time you told someone about the reality of sin and hell and his need for forgiveness? Did you tell him in a spirit of loving concern? Do you think he sensed it? What was his reaction? How would you approach someone who is fascinated with Jesus as opposed to someone who is hostile toward Him? If a person continued to reject the gospel and you therefore chose not to cast your pearls before swine (Matt. 7:6), that

doesn't necessarily mean that you have to reject that person as a friend. God may soften his heart. Consistently pray for that individual, and be willing to interact with him so that your life can reflect the love of Christ to him.

Moody Press, a ministry of the Moody Bible Institute, is designed for education, evangelization, and edification. If we may assist you in knowing more about Christ and the Christian life, please write us without obligation: Moody Press, c/o MLM, Chicago, IL 60610.

Scripture Index

143